CRITICAL THINKING USING PRIMARY SOURCES IN U.S. HISTORY

WENDY S. WILSON AND
GERALD H. HERMAN

J. WESTON

WALCH
PUBLISHER

User's Guide
to
Walch Reproducible Books

As part of our general effort to provide educational materials that are as practical and economical as possible, we have designated this publication a "reproducible book." The designation means that purchase of the book includes purchase of the right to limited reproduction of all pages on which this symbol appears:

Here is the basic Walch policy: We grant to individual purchasers of this book the right to make sufficient copies of reproducible pages for use by all students of a single teacher. This permission is limited to a single teacher and does not apply to entire schools or school systems, so institutions purchasing the book should pass the permission on to a single teacher. Copying of the book or its parts for resale is prohibited.

Any questions regarding this policy or requests to purchase further reproduction rights should be addressed to:

Permissions Editor
J. Weston Walch, Publisher
321 Valley Street
P.O. Box 658
Portland, Maine 04104-0658

1   2   3   4   5   6   7   8   9   10
ISBN 0-8251-4144-3

Copyright © 2000
J. Weston Walch, Publisher
P.O. Box 658 • Portland, Maine 04104-0658
www.walch.com

Printed in the United States of America

Contents

To the Teacher

One of the most essential skills we can teach our students is **critical reading**, which includes **critical thinking** through the evaluation of source materials, particularly primary sources. This significant skill is included in many state frameworks, and it constitutes an important section of the advanced placement examinations employing DBQs, or document-based assessment questions.

The ability to read a complex document, to glean significant facts from it, and to detect and analyze any inherent biases and misstatements is a competency clearly needed by all our students, regardless of their ability level or the historical era (including the present day) under study. In fact, in our technological age, the deluge of information available on the World Wide Web and elsewhere, makes even more urgent this capacity to determine the relative accuracy and merits of a given document. That is the principle around which this reproducible book is framed.

To accomplish this end, the authors have used figures from a broad range of times and cultures in American history who have helped to shape the period in which they lived. Each unit of this book focuses on one of these individuals.

Materials Included in This Book

Units include the following reproducible materials for your students:

- extensive **background information** on the person and historical era being highlighted
- **key questions** for students to consider as they engage in critical reading about this person and his or her time
- fascinating **primary sources** (letters, eyewitness accounts, diary entries, autobiographical extracts, artwork, government documents, congressional and parliamentary proceedings, and other authentic narratives)

- carefully selected **secondary sources** (magazine and newspaper articles, historical texts, and other nonfiction accounts)
- a detailed list of **multimedia resources** for further investigation
- suggested "charges" for an optional **mock trial**

Suggested Procedure for Each Unit

Each unit begins with a reproducible **Historical Background** section. You may decide to assign this section for home reading, or you can have students read the information in class.

The Historical Background reading is followed by **Key Questions** for students to consider as they read through the documents that follow. These questions will help them understand the historical context surrounding the person and the events highlighted in the unit. The questions will also help students grasp differing points of view (both political and cultural) that may have affected the events being described. Key questions can be answered in a number of ways: (1) orally, within the framework of a whole-class discussion; (2) orally, with individual students or small groups of students answering a question assigned by the teacher; or (3) in writing, with students responding to specific questions in either essay or short-answer format.

The Key Questions are followed by a suggestion for a **Mock Trial**, should you and your students decide to engage in a more "hands-on" activity to extend the unit. (See heading below.)

The section titled **Documents** contains all of the reproducible readings that have been selected to present the person and topic under study. You may wish to exclude one or more of the documents in each unit, depending on your students' reading abilities and/or the time you have allotted for this activity. You may also choose to assign each document to a small group of students to read and analyze together; groups can then report on their individual documents in a jigsaw-style activity.

A **list of possible Resources** for each unit follows the Documents section; you may wish to use these Resources to extend your students' understanding of the issues. In a very few cases, some suggested movies are not currently in distribution. However, these movies are occasionally shown in theaters or on TV, and they are excellent Resources, if available.

The Teacher Guide at the end of this volume includes **Key Features of Documents Used in This Book** to help you in assessing whether your students have grasped the most salient points in each of the documents you have assigned.

Mock Trials

A number of sensational trials have dominated the popular media in recent history. How can we, as teachers, turn our nation's fascination with trials into a learning experience? One way is to involve our students in an investigative exercise that encourages them to participate in the information gathering and critical evaluation of evidence necessary to prepare for a mock trial. This format helps students develop their research skills, learn to present information (testimony) clearly, and improve their critical-thinking skills in the evaluation of primary source materials (evidence) to formulate a conclusion or verdict.

The reproducible pages in the Mock Trials section at the back of this book will help you and your students prepare for a trial. If your school has a mock trial club, you might enlist members' support in setting up your trial scenario.

Each unit in this book includes a suggested "charge" to be brought against the featured person. In addition, the Mock Trials section contains possible witness lists. The primary documents included in the unit can be used as evidence; you may also choose to add other documents or items to supplement those provided in the book.

Other Options

Teachers pressed for time can use the trial charges and documents for independent research assignments. Or, a class could debate the culpability of the historical figure. Both the trial and the debate formats offer excellent performance-based assessment options. And, no matter how the material is used, students learn to evaluate their sources and view all information with a critical eye. We hope that you and your students enjoy these materials.

About the Authors

Wendy S. Wilson has been a teacher in the Lexington, Massachusetts, public schools since 1971. She has taught social studies in grades 7–12, was appointed interim social studies department head, and served as the cable television specialist system-wide. She is also a senior lecturer in history at University College, Northeastern University, and team-teaches a graduate course in history and media with Gerald Herman. She is a frequent presenter at conferences and in other professional development activities. She is the coauthor of several other Walch publications, *American History on the Screen* with Gerald Herman, *Ellis Island and Beyond* and *Heading West* with Jack Papadonis, and *Native Americans* with Lloyd Thompson.

Gerald H. Herman is a tenured assistant professor of history and special assistant to the office of the general counsel at Northeastern University. He has also served as acting department chair of the history department. He is the author of a nine-part multimedia presentation and anthology on the culture of world war entitled *World War I: The Destroying Fathers Confirmed,* and of an award-winning National Public Radio program on the same subject called *War*. He has also written extensively on history and film, including analyses of individual films, teacher guides for both secondary schools and colleges, and bibliographical references, and currently serves as media editor for *The Public Historian*. He has completed work on a radio exploration of the culture of World War II entitled *The Sound in the Fury* for National Public Radio and is writing a comprehensive *Historians' Guide to Films*.

The authors wish to thank Jeremy Niell and Brynn Thompson of the Northeastern University History Department for their help in researching and compiling the materials in this book.

UNIT 1 | Christopher Columbus and the New World

HISTORICAL BACKGROUND

Christopher Columbus, more accurately known as Cristoforo Colombo or Cristóbal Colón, was born either in or near Genoa, Italy, in 1451. He was the son of a weaver and probably worked with his father at the craft from an early age. Columbus sailed on a trading mission to Flanders in 1476, but the ship he was on was sunk by the French off the Portuguese coast at Lagos. Columbus managed to swim ashore and proceeded to travel 160 miles to Lisbon, where his brother Bartholomé was working. Lisbon at that time was a very important center for European exploration and navigation.

In Lisbon, Columbus worked as a merchant seaman and sailed to the British Isles and perhaps Iceland. He met with enough success to be able to marry a lady of an upstanding family of the Madeira Islands. He settled in the Madeiras and made more voyages as a traveling merchant. At this time Columbus probably taught himself how to read and write and learned some Latin, Spanish, and Portuguese. He also studied the new printed materials on navigation and many of the maps being produced. Columbus became convinced that a shortcut to Asia lay in going west across the Atlantic Ocean. Columbus tried many different times to interest European powers in supporting his voyage of exploration to the west. He approached the king of Portugal as well as monarchs of Spain (Castile), England, and France. Finally, in 1492, Isabella and Ferdinand of Spain agreed to sponsor Columbus. He received three ships for his expedition, money for crew and supplies, the right to receive ten percent of any trade he began, and the governorship over any new land. In August of 1492, Columbus and his expedition set sail for Asia.

In October 1492, Columbus arrived on land that he assumed was one of the outer islands of Cipangu (Japan). Upon going ashore, Columbus claimed the land for the king and queen of Spain and met the natives, whom he referred to as Indians, since he supposed he was in the East Indies. Columbus took seven natives as prisoners and hoped that they would lead him to the grand khan (emperor of China) and the gold Columbus hoped to find. Instead, he discovered the island of Cuba and then sailed to an island that he named Española, where his flagship, the Santa Maria, hit a reef. The local chieftain, or cacique, of the island, Guacanagari, sent Columbus presents, which included some items of gold. Guacanagari also helped Columbus salvage supplies from his foundering ship. Columbus used the timbers from the abandoned ship to build a fort on the island, which he called Puerto de Navidad. To awe the natives into submission, Columbus fired rounds from his cannons, which terrified the cacique and his people.

In January 1493, 38 men were left to defend the fort. Columbus sailed for home, taking with him some Taino Indians to be shown to the Spanish rulers. Upon reporting to the king and queen about his findings, which he embellished to include such riches as spices and precious metals, Columbus received the title "Admiral of the Ocean Sea, Viceroy and Governor of the islands he has discovered in the Indies." A second expedition was mounted that year with 17

Critical Thinking Using Primary Sources in U.S. History

ships, which carried supplies, animals, and over a thousand men, some with their families.

Columbus explored some of the islands of the Lesser Antilles, but ultimately he returned to La Navidad on Española, known today as the Dominican Republic and Haiti. He found the fort abandoned and the men he had left there, dead. The soldiers had enslaved the Taino women and mistreated the Indians and had been killed in reprisal. Columbus explored the eastern part of Española and found some sources of gold in an area called Cibao. Desperate to turn a profit and prove to the Spanish crown that his voyage was fruitful, Columbus forced the Tainos to pay a tribute every three months to the Spanish consisting of enough gold dust to fill a hawk's bell. He also shipped Indians to Spain to be sold as slaves. During this second voyage to the New World, Columbus often left the small Spanish colony of Española in the hands of others, such as his brother Diego, and went to explore the other islands.

In 1496, Columbus sailed back to Spain to defend his reputation against detractors who accused him of poor administration and of not producing the spices and gold he had promised. Despite a rather lukewarm welcome, Columbus did receive funding to go on a third voyage and left Spain in May 1498. Three of his six ships went directly to Española, but Columbus took three ships and explored what is today Trinidad and the coastline of South America. Columbus then returned to Española, which he found in chaos. The colony was suffering from illness, hunger, and infighting among the Spanish. The royal government sent out a commissioner to try to restore order. Columbus and his brothers, Diego and Bartholomé, were arrested and sent back to Spain shackled in irons in 1500.

After two years of pleading his case, Columbus was given permission by the Spanish monarchs to try once more to find China. In 1502, he set sail with four worm-eaten ships and tried to land at Española, where permission was denied by the present governor. Columbus then explored the coast of Central America and landed in Panama. He was also marooned on the island of Jamaica for a year. Finally, the company was rescued by a relief ship and made their way to Española. In September 1504, Columbus returned to Spain. He spent the last two years of his life writing letters to the Spanish court complaining of his treatment. In 1506, Columbus died at Valladolid, Spain.

Key Questions About This Subject

- What was Columbus' reason for undertaking his voyage west across the Atlantic Ocean?
- Upon his discovery of the islands of the Caribbean and the indigenous peoples there, how did Columbus attempt to make this venture worthwhile to his sponsors, the king and queen of Spain?
- Can Columbus be held personally accountable for the devastation visited upon the indigenous peoples by the Spaniards?
- What was the most serious calamity to befall the indigenous peoples of the Americas?

- Who was responsible for this? Could anyone be declared morally responsible?
- Were the actions of the Spanish any more cruel and reprehensible than those that the native leaders (such as the Aztec chiefs and priests) inflicted upon their own people?
- Given that Europeans would eventually have reached the Western Hemisphere, and given the conditions of the fifteenth and sixteenth centuries, can you see any scenario in which Europeans and Native Americans could have met and established peaceful relations?

2 *Critical Thinking Using Primary Sources in U.S. History*

Mock Trial

If you are going to hold a simulated trial, here are the charges against Christopher Columbus (the Defendant): Christopher Columbus, a Genoese seaman in the service of King Ferdinand and Queen Isabella of Spain, is accused of crimes against humanity and the environment, in that he and his men were responsible for the deaths of many of the indigenous people referred to by Columbus as "Indians." Columbus also stands accused of causing ecological devastation through the importing of plant and animal life not native to the Western Hemisphere.

DOCUMENTS

Document A

A Letter to Lord Sanchez, 1493

(From *Select Letters of Christopher Columbus,* translated and edited by R.H. Hajor. London: The Hakluyt Society, 1847, pp. 6–10. As found in Dennis Sherman, ed., *Western Civilization: Sources, Images, and Interpretation from the Renaissance to the Present.* New York: McGraw-Hill, 1995, pp. 53–54.)

The inhabitants of both sexes in this island, and in all the others which I have seen, or of which I have received information, go always naked as they were born, with the exception of some of the women, who use the covering of leaf, or small bough, or an apron of cotton which they prepare for that purpose. None of them . . . are possessed of any iron, neither have they weapons, being unacquainted with, and indeed incompetent to use them, not from any deformity of body (for they are well-formed), but because they are timid and full of fear. . . . This timidity did not arise from any loss or injury that they received from us; for on the contrary, I gave to all I approached whatever articles I had about me, such as cloth and many other things, taking nothing of theirs in return: but they are naturally timid and fearful. As soon however as they see that they are safe, and have laid aside all fear, they are very simple and honest, and exceedingly liberal with all they have; none of them refusing any thing he may possess when he is asked for it, but on the contrary inviting us to ask them. They exhibit great love towards all others in preference to themselves: they also give objects of great value for trifles, and content themselves with very little or nothing in return. I however forbad that these trifles and articles of no value (such as pieces of dishes, plates, and glass, keys, and leather straps) should be given to them, although if they could obtain them, they imagined themselves to be possessed of the most beautiful trinkets in the world. . . . Thus they bartered, like idiots, cotton and gold for fragments of bows, glasses, bottles, and jars; which I forbad as being unjust, and myself gave them many beautiful and acceptable articles which I had brought with me, taking nothing from them in return; I did this in order that I might the more easily conciliate them, that they might be led to become Christians, and might be inclined to entertain a regard for the King and Queen, our Princes and all Spaniards, and that I might induce them to take an interest in seeking out, and collecting, and delivering to us such things as they possessed in abundance, but which we greatly needed. . . . On my arrival at that sea, I had taken some Indians by force from the first island that I came to, in order that they might learn our language and communicate to us what they knew respecting the country; which plan succeeded excellently, and was a great advantage to us. . . . In all these islands there is no difference of physiognomy, of manners, or of language, but they all clearly understand each other, a circumstance very propitious for the realization of what I conceive to be the principal wish of our most serene King, namely, the conversion of these people to the holy faith of Christ, to which indeed, as far as I can judge, they are very favourable and well-disposed.

Document B

Hispaniola

(From Bartolomé de las Casas, *The Devastation of the Indies.* Baltimore: Johns Hopkins University Press, 1992, pp. 32–35. Originally published in Spanish in 1552.)

On the island of Hispaniola was where the Spaniards first landed, as I have said. Here those Christians perpetrated their first ravages and oppressions against the native peoples. This was the first land in the New World to be destroyed and depopulated by the Christians, and here they began their subjection of the women and children, taking them away from the Indians to use them and ill use them, eating the food they provided with their sweat and toil. The Spaniards did not content themselves with what the Indians gave them of their own free will, according to their ability, which was always too little to satisfy enormous appetites, for a Christian eats and consumes in one day an amount of food that would suffice to feed three houses inhabited by ten Indians for one month. And they committed other acts of force and violence and oppression which made the Indians realize that these men had not come from Heaven. And some of the Indians concealed their foods while others concealed their wives and children and still others fled to the mountains to avoid the terrible transactions of the Christians. . . .

From that time onward the Indians began to seek ways to throw the Christians out of their lands. They took up arms, but their weapons were very weak and of little service in offense and still less in defense. And the Christians, with their horses and swords and pikes began to carry out massacres and strange cruelties against them. They attacked the towns and spared neither the children nor the aged nor pregnant women nor women in childbed, not only stabbing them and dismembering them but cutting them to pieces as if dealing with sheep in the slaughter house. They laid bets as to who, with one stroke of the sword, could split a man in two or could cut off his head or spill out his entrails with a single stroke of the pike. They took infants from their mothers' breasts, snatching them by the legs and pitching them headfirst against the crags or snatched them by the arms and threw them into the rivers, roaring with laughter and saying as the babies fell into the water, "Boil there, you offspring of the devil!" Other infants they put to the sword along with their mothers and anyone else who happened to be nearby. . . . They usually dealt with the chieftains and nobles in the following way: they made a grid of rods which they placed on forked sticks, then lashed the victims to the grid and lighted a smoldering fire underneath, so that little by little, as those captives screamed in despair and torment, their souls would leave them.

Document C

The Great Disease Migration

(From Cowley, Geoffrey, "The Great Disease Migration," *Newsweek,* Special Issue, Fall/Winter, 1991. pp. 54–56.)

. . . Many experts now believe that the New World was home to 40 million to 50 million people before Columbus arrived and that most of them died within decades. In Mexico alone, the native population fell from roughly 30 million in 1519 to 3 million in 1568. There was similar devastation throughout the Caribbean islands, Central America and Peru. The eminent Yale historian David Brion Davis says this was "the greatest genocide in the history of man." Yet it's increasingly clear that most of the carnage had nothing to do with European barbarism. The worst of the suffering was caused not by swords or guns but by germs.

Contrary to popular belief, viruses, bacteria and other invisible parasites aren't designed to cause harm; they fare best in the struggle to survive and reproduce when they don't destroy their hosts. But when a new germ invades a previously unexposed population, it often causes devastating epidemics, killing all but the most resistant individuals. . . .

By the time Columbus set sail, the people of the Old World held the distinction of being thoroughly diseased. By domesticating pigs, horses, sheep and cattle, they had infected themselves with a wide array of pathogens. And through centuries of war, exploration, and city-building, they had kept those agents in constant circulation. Virtually any European who crossed the Atlantic during the 16th century had battled such illnesses as smallpox and measles during childhood and emerged fully immune.

By contrast, the people of the Americas had spent thousands of years in biological isolation. . . . By the time Columbus had arrived, groups like the Aztecs and Maya of Central America and Peru's Incas had built cities large enough to sustain major epidemics. Archeological evidence suggests they suffered from syphilis, tuberculosis, a few intestinal parasites and some types of influenza (probably those carried by waterfowl). Yet they remained untouched by diseases that had raged for centuries in the Old World. When the newcomers arrived carrying mumps, measles, whooping cough, smallpox, cholera, gonorrhea and yellow fever, the Indians were immunologically defenseless.

An illustration of an Aztec human sacrifice (located at the Museo de la Ciudad de Mexico, Mexico City)

© Gianni Dagli Orti/CORBIS

The Aztecs believed that the gods who had created the world needed human blood to sustain it. Hearts were removed from the victims' chests and offered as a sacrifice to the sun.

The Aztecs

(From the Editors of Time-Life Books, *Aztecs: Reign of Blood and Splendor*. Alexandria, VA: Time-Life Books, 1992, pp. 82–83.)

Driven by fear of the gods, particularly Huitzilopouchtli, the Aztecs performed human sacrifice on a scale unknown either before or since in history. The conquistador Bernal Diaz del Castillo was an eyewitness to this bloodletting and wrote vividly of the fate of some of his friends, whom the Aztecs had captured during the climactic battle between the Indians and the Spaniards for control of the city in the spring of 1521. From the place to which Diaz had been forced to retreat, he could see the temple. At the terrifying sound of the Huitzilopouchtli shrine drum, which was accompanied by the blare of conchs, horns, and trumpetlike instruments, Diaz glanced toward the Great Temple and saw that some of his comrades, who had been captured by the Aztecs, were being dragged to the top to be sacrificed. When the Indians had gotten them "to a small square where their accursed idols are kept," recounted Diaz in the breathless style of someone who has beheld horror and never been able to forget it, "we saw them place plumes on the head of many of our men and with things like fans in their hands they forced them to dance before Huitzilopouchtli, and after they had danced they placed them on their backs on some rather narrow stones which had been prepared as places for sacrifice, and with stone knives they sawed open their chests and drew out their palpitating hearts and offered them to the idols that were there, and they kicked the bodies down the steps, and Indian butchers who were waiting below cut off the arms and feet and flayed the skin off the faces, and prepared it afterward like glove leather with the beards on, and kept those for the festivals when they celebrated drunken orgies, and the flesh they ate with chilies."

Critical Thinking Using
Primary Sources in U.S. History

Resources

Bibliography

Barden, Renardo. *The Discovery of America*. San Diego: Greenhaven Press, 1991.

Bigelow, Bill, et al., ed. *Rethinking Columbus*. Milwaukee: Rethinking Schools, Ltd., 1991.

"Columbus: Will the Hero of 1492 Be the Villain of 1992?" *Time*, October 7, 1991, pp. 52–61.

Crosby, Alfred W. *The Columbian Exchange: Biological and Cultural Consequences of 1492*. Westport, CT: Greenwood Press, 1972.

de las Casas, Bartolomé. *The Devastation of the Indies*. Baltimore: Johns Hopkins University Press, 1992.

de las Casas, Bartolomé. *The Log of Christopher Columbus' First Voyage to America*. North Haven, CT: Linnet Books, 1989.

Dor-Ner, Zvi. *Columbus and the Age of Discovery*. New York: Morrow, 1991.

Dyson, John. *Columbus: For Gold, God, and Glory*. New York: Simon & Schuster, 1991.

Fernandes-Arnesto, Felipe. *Columbus*. New York: Oxford University Press, 1991.

Funson, Robert H., translator. *The Log of Christopher Columbus*. Camden, ME: International Marine Publishing/TAB Books, 1987.

Gray, P. "The Trouble with Columbus," *Time*, October 7, 1991, pp. 52–56.

Hawke, Sharryl, and James Davis. *Seeds of Change: The Story of the Cultural Exchange After 1492*. Boston: Addison-Wesley, 1992.

Hughes, H. "Just Who Was That Man?" *Time*, October 7, 1991, pp. 58–59.

Josephy, Alvin M., Jr. *America in 1492*. New York: Alfred A. Knopf, 1992.

Keen, Benjamin, translator. *The Life of the Admiral Christopher Columbus by His Son Ferdinand*. New Brunswick, NJ: Rutgers University Press, 1950.

Koning, Hans. *Columbus: His Enterprise*. New York: Monthly Review Press, 1991.

Lunenfeld, Marvin, ed. *1492: Discovery, Invasion, Encounter*. Lexington, MA: D.C. Heath, 1991.

Meltzer, Milton. *Columbus and the World Around Him*. New York: Franklin Watts, 1990.

Milanich, Jerald T., and Susan Milbrath, ed. *First Encounters: Spanish Explorations in the Caribbean and the United States*. Gainesville: University of Florida Press, 1989.

Morison, Samuel Eliot. *Admiral of the Ocean Sea: A Life of Christopher Columbus*. Boston: Northeastern University Press, 1983.

National Geographic, October 1991.

Pelta, Kathy. *Discovering Christopher Columbus: How History Is Invented*. Minneapolis: Lerner Publications, 1991.

Sale, Kirkpatrick. *The Conquest of Paradise: Christopher Columbus and the Columbian Legacy*. New York: Alfred A. Knopf, 1990.

Smith, Richard M., ed. "When Worlds Collide: Columbus Special Issue."*Newsweek,* Fall/Winter, 1991.

Viola, Herman, and Carolyn Margolis, ed. *Seeds of Change: A Quincentennial Commemoration*. Washington, DC: Smithsonian Institution Press, 1991.

Weatherford, Jack. *Indian Givers, How the Indians of the Americas Transformed the World*. New York: Crown Publishers, 1988.

Wilford, John Noble. "Discovering Columbus." *New York Times Magazine*, August 11, 1991, pp. 24–29, 45–47, 55.

Wilford, John Noble. *The Mysterious History of Columbus: An Exploration of the Man, the Myth, the Legacy*. New York: Alfred A. Knopf, 1991.

Media Resources

Documentaries

Christopher Columbus and the Great Adventure. 28 minutes. Video Knowledge, 1991. Good overview of the Columbus voyages and their impact on the peoples of the Americas. Available from Zenger Media, 800-421-4246.

Columbus and the Age of Discovery. 60 minutes each part. PBS, 1990. This seven-part series produced for the Columbus quincentennial is highly recommended. Presently out of distribution, but possibly available in public school libraries.

500 Nations. 49 minutes each part. Columbia House, 1994. Eight-part series exploring various aspects of native North American culture. The first three programs are pertinent to the time of Columbus. Available as a set or as separate videos from Zenger Media, 800-421-4246.

Feature Films

Christopher Columbus. 135 minutes. Warner Home Video, 1985. Originally 360 minutes, this two-part Italian-U.S. television miniseries has been edited for general distribution.

Christopher Columbus: The Discovery. 120 minutes. 1992. Directed by Alexander Salkind, this film concerns the efforts of Columbus to convince the Spanish monarchs to sponsor his voyage. Includes a fictional meeting between Columbus and the grand inquisitor, Torquemada, played by Marlon Brando. Available in many video stores.

1492: Conquest of Paradise. 152 minutes. 1992. Directed by Ridley Scott and starring Gerard Depardieu as Columbus. Available at many video stores.

UNIT 2 | Samuel Adams and the American Revolution

HISTORICAL BACKGROUND

Samuel Adams was born in Boston in 1722. His father, also named Samuel, was a prosperous businessman and an important figure at the Old South Meetinghouse, and thus was referred to as Deacon Adams. At 14, young Samuel Adams entered Harvard, as befitted the son of a Boston dignitary. There are no records of his academic career, but it is probable that at Harvard Adams became familiar with John Locke's treatise *Of Civil Government*. In this treatise, Locke set out his doctrine that every citizen had natural rights of life, liberty, and property, and that a ruler could not take property from his subjects in the form of taxation without their consent.

Adams graduated from Harvard in 1740 and went on to receive his master's degree in 1743. Deacon Adams had hoped that his son would become a merchant, but he had suffered some financial reverses, and young Samuel showed little interest in business. In 1748, Deacon Adams died, and Samuel inherited his father's business, which supplied malt to brewers. Under Samuel's control the business soon declined. What really came to interest Samuel Adams was politics. By 1763, he had joined the Caucus Club. This was a secret organization that met in advance of all town meetings to decide upon the slate of candidates for office and what the stands would be on various issues.

In 1764, Adams was given the responsibility of writing the instructions for Boston's representatives to the provincial legislature. In 1765, the British Parliament had passed the Stamp Act, which required the purchase of a stamp on every legal and business document. Adams led the outcry against this act and encouraged the representatives to refuse to accept this tax. Until then, Parliament had passed laws to govern seaborne trade, and the colonies were pretty much left to govern themselves. Now, the British government felt that the expense of maintaining the empire in North America should be shared by the colonists. Thus, they began to devise plans for direct taxation. Adams became the most outspoken opponent of this form of taxation; he was looked upon as the leader of the "patriots" who opposed parliamentary control over the colonies.

In 1765, Adams was elected to the Massachusetts Legislature, where he served until 1774. After 1768, Adams became a frequent contributor to the Boston newspapers and wrote often to oppose the policies of the colonial governor and Parliament. At this early date, Adams did not advocate separation of the colonies from England.

Although Parliament had repealed the Stamp Act in 1766, it next passed the Townshend Acts, which required import duties on paint, glass, paper, and tea. Once again, Adams rose to head the opposition and organized merchants into the Non-importation Association. He wrote a letter to other colonial assemblies condemning British policy. The British sent troops to Boston to maintain the peace, and Adams spoke out against this presence in his town.

Critical Thinking Using
Primary Sources in U.S. History

In March 1770, a mob taunted British soldiers on duty at the custom house. Eventually, the soldiers fired into the mob, killing three men and wounding many others. This became known as the "Boston Massacre" and led Adams to send a delegation to Lt. Governor Hutchinson asking that the troops be removed from Boston. Hutchinson gave in. Because of the agitation, the Townshend duties were repealed, except for the tax on tea.

While the unrest abated, Adams kept on writing newspaper articles warning that colonial liberties were at risk. In 1773, when Parliament gave the East India Company the monopoly of the tea trade in America, Adams demanded that three ships carrying the tea be ordered to return to England. At a town meeting, Adams received word that Hutchinson (who was now governor) refused his demand. Adams then announced that "This meeting can do nothing more to save the country." Fifty to a hundred men disguised as Indians boarded the three ships and dumped tea into Boston Harbor.

Britain sought to punish Boston by issuing the Intolerable or Coercive Acts of 1774. These Acts closed the port of Boston, sent troops to the town, and moved the provincial capital and assembly to Salem. At the assembly, Adams kept the doors to the chamber locked so that the governor could not dissolve it before representatives could be elected to the First Continental Congress. Adams was one of the elected members. Adams then worked for the adoption of the "Suffolk Resolves," which put Massachusetts in a state of rebellion, and lobbied the Continental Congress for their acceptance. Adams signed the Declaration of Independence as a member of the Second Continental Congress in Philadelphia.

Adams went on to serve in various offices, including in Congress, in the state senate, and as governor of Massachusetts. He retired from public life in 1797 and died in Boston in 1803.

Key Questions About This Subject

- Why did the British government feel that taxing the American colonies was reasonable, particularly after 1763, the end of the French and Indian War?
- Why did Britain's increasing control over the colonies seem to the colonists like a dramatic change in policy?
- Why were colonial merchants particularly angered by the taxes and restrictions imposed by the British?
- How might the economic theory of mercantilism contribute to the frustration of the colonists?
- What was the cause of the "Boston Tea Party," and what was the result?

- Upon what historical basis did the colonists claim that they were subject to "taxation without representation?"
- How did Sam Adams and other leaders justify rebellion against the English monarch?
- Was there any precedent for rebellion against a monarch who violated "natural rights"?
- Was the outbreak of hostilities between the American colonists and the British authorities truly a question of "natural rights," or was it based on economic self-interest?

Mock Trial

If you are going to hold a simulated trial, here are the charges against Samuel Adams (the Defendant): Samuel Adams, resident of Boston in His Majesty's colony of Massachusetts, is charged with inciting revolt against the rule of George III. Adams is further charged with the destruction of private property by dumping shipments of tea into Boston Harbor.

DOCUMENTS

Document A

Boston Massacre, March 5, 1770

Eyewitness Account of the Boston Tea Party, by Robert Sessions

(From Wesley S. Griswald, *The Night the Revolution Began.* N.P.: Stephen Greene Press, 1972. As found in Milton Meltzer, *The American Revolutionaries: A History in Their Own Words, 1750–1800.* New York: Thomas Y. Crowell, 1987, pp. 50–51.)

I was living in Boston at the time, in the family of a Mr. Davis, a lumber merchant, as a common laborer. On that eventful evening, when Mr. Davis came in from the town meeting, I asked him what was to be done with the tea.

"They are now throwing it overboard," he replied.

Receiving permission, I went immediately to the spot. Everything was as light as day, by the means of lamps and torches—a pin might be seen lying on the wharf. I went on board where they were at work, and took hold with my own hands.

I was not one of those appointed to destroy the tea, and who disguised themselves as Indians, but was a volunteer, the disguised men being largely men of family and position in Boston, while I was a young man whose home and relations were in Connecticut. The appointed and disguised party proving too small for the quick work necessary, other young men, similarly circumstanced with myself, joined them in their labors.

The chests were drawn up by a tackle—one man bringing them forward in the hold, another putting a rope around them, and others hoisting them to the deck and carrying them to the vessel's side. The chests were then opened, the tea emptied over the side, and the chests thrown overboard.

Perfect regularity prevailed during the whole transaction. Although there were many people on the wharf, entire silence prevailed—no clamor, no talking. Nothing was meddled with but the teas on board.

After having emptied the hold, the deck was swept clean, and everything put in its proper place. An officer on board was requested to come up from the cabin and see that no damage was done except to the tea.

John Adams Reflects on the Boston Tea Party, 1773

(From L.H. Butterfield, ed., *Diary and Autobiography of John Adams.* Cambridge, MA: Belknap Press of the Harvard University Press and the Massachusetts Historical Society, 1961. As found in Richard D. Brown, ed., *Major Problems in the Era of the American Revolution, 1760–1791.* Lexington, MA: D.C. Heath, 1992, p. 132.)

Last Night 3 Cargoes of Bohea Tea were emptied into the Sea. This Morning a Man of War sails.

This is the most magnificent Movement of all. There is a Dignity, a Majesty, a Sublimity, in this last Effort of the Patriots, that I greatly admire. The People should never rise, without doing something to be remembered—something notable And striking. This Destruction of the Tea is so bold, so daring, so firm, intrepid and inflexible, and it must have so important Consequences, and so lasting, that I cant but consider it as an Epocha in History.

This however is but an Attack upon Property. Another similar Exertion of popular Power, may produce the destruction of Lives. Many Person wish, that as many dead Carcasses were floating in the Harbour, as there are Chests of Tea:—a much less Number of Lives however would remove the Causes of all our Calamities. . . .

What Measures will the Ministry take, in Consequence of this?—Will they resent it? will they dare to resent it? will they punish Us? How? By quartering Troops upon Us?—by annulling our Charter?—by laying on more duties? By restraining our Trade? By Sacrifice of Individuals, or how.

The Question is whether the Destruction of this Tea was necessary? I apprehend it was absolutely and indispensably so.—They could not send it back, the Governor, Admiral and Collector and Comptroller would not suffer it. It was in their Power to have saved it—but in no other. It could not get by the Castle, the Men of War &c. Then there was no other Alternative but to destroy it or let it be landed. To let it be landed, would be giving up the Principle of Taxation by Parliamentary Authority, against which the Continent have struggled for 10 years, it was loosing all our labour for 10 years and subjecting ourselves and our Posterity forever to Egyptian Taskmasters—to Burthens, Indignities, to Ignominy, Reproach and Contempt, to Desolation and Oppression, to Poverty and Servitude.

But it will be said it might have been left in the Care of a Committee of the Town, or in Castle William. To this many Objections may be made.

Deacon Palmer and Mr. Is. Smith dined with me, and Mr. Trumble came in. They say, the Tories blame the Consignees, as much as the Whiggs do—and say that the Governor will loose his Place, for not taking the Tea into his Protection before, by Means of the Ships of War, I suppose, and the Troops at the Castle.

Document D

George Grenville Defends the Stamp Act in Parliamentary Debate with William Pitt, January 14, 1766

(From *Hansard's Parliamentary Debates*, Vol. XVI, 1766, pp. 98–107. As found in Blanche M. Touhill, *Readings in American History*. River Forest, IL: Laidlaw Brothers, 1970, p. 39–40.)

. . . I cannot understand the difference between external and internal taxes. They are the same in effect, and only differ in name. That his [the King of England's] kingdom has the sovereign, the supreme legislative power over America, is granted. It cannot be denied; and taxation is a part of that sovereign power. It is one branch of the legislation. It is, it has been exercised, over those who are not, who were never presented. It is exercised over the India Company, the merchants of London, the proprietors of the stocks, and over many great manufacturing towns.

Critical Thinking Using
Primary Sources in U.S. History

It was exercised over the Palatinate of Chester, and the bishopric of Durham, before they sent any representatives to parliament. . . . When I proposed to tax America, I asked the House, if any gentleman would object to the right; I repeatedly asked it and no man would attempt to deny it. Protection and obedience are reciprocal. Great Britain protects America; America is bound to yield to obedience. If not, tell me when the Americans were emancipated? When they want the protection of this kingdom, they are always very ready to ask it. That protection has always been afforded them in the most full and ample manner. The nation has run itself into an immense debt to give them their protection; and now they are called upon to contribute a small share towards the public expense, an expense arising from themselves, they renounce your authority, insult your officers, and break out, I might almost say, into open rebellion. The seditious spirit of the colonies owes its birth to the factions in this House. Gentlemen are careless of the consequences of what they say, provided it answers the purposes of opposition. We were told we trod on tender ground; we were bid to expect disobedience. What was this, but telling the Americans to stand out against the law, to encourage their obstinacy with the expectation of support from hence? Let us only hold out a little, they would say, our friends will soon be in power. Ungrateful people of America! Bounties have been extended to them. . . .

Document E

From Governor Hutchinson's *History of Massachusetts-Bay*

(From Henry Steel Commager and Richard B. Morris, ed., *The Spirit of Seventy-six: The Story of the American Revolution As Told by Participants.* New York: Harper & Row, 1967, p.10.)

This [the Tea Party] was the boldest stroke which had yet been struck in America. The people in all parts of the province shewed more or less concern at the expected consequences. They were, however, at a distance; something might intervene to divert them. Besides, the thing was done: there was no way of nullifying it. Their leaders feared no consequences. To engage the people in some desperate measure had long been their plan. They never discovered more concern than when the people were quiet upon the repeal of an act of Parliament, or upon concessions made or assurances given; and never more satisfaction than when government had taken any new measures, or appeared to be inclined to them, tending, or which might be improved, to irritate and disturb the people. They had nothing to fear for themselves. They had gone too far to recede. If the colonies were subject to the supreme authority and laws of Great Britain, their offences, long since, had been of the highest nature. Their all depended upon attaining to the object which first engaged them. There was no way of attaining to it but by involving the body of the people in the same circumstances they were in themselves. And it is certain that ever after this time an opinion was easily instilled, and was continually increasing, that the body of the people had also gone too far to recede, and that an open and general revolt must be the consequence; and it was not long before actual preparations were visibly making for it in most parts of the province.

Critical Thinking Using
Primary Sources in U.S. History

Resources

Bibliography

Bailyn, Bernard. *The Ordeal of Thomas Hutchinson.* Cambridge, MA: Harvard University Press, 1976.

Beach, Stewart. *Samuel Adams: The Fateful Years, 1764–1776.* New York: Dodd, Mead & Company, 1965.

Brown, Richard D., ed. *Major Problems in the Era of the American Revolution, 1760–1791.* Lexington, MA: D.C. Heath, 1992.

Commager, Henry Steele, and Richard B. Morris, eds. *The Spirit of Seventy-six: The Story of the American Revolution As Told by Participants.* New York: Harper & Row, 1967.

Fowler, William M., Jr. *Samuel Adams: Radical Puritan.* New York: Addison Wesley, 1997.

Fowler, William M., Jr., and Wallace Coyle, eds. *The American Revolution: Changing Perspectives.* Boston, MA: Northeastern University Press, 1979.

Labaree, Benjamin W. *The Boston Tea Party.* Boston: Northeastern University, 1979.

Maier, Pauline. *From Resistance to Revolution: Colonial Radicals and the Development of American Opposition to Britain.* New York: W.W. Norton, 1992 (reprint edition).

Meltzer, Milton. *The American Revolutionaries: A History in Their Own Words, 1750–1800.* New York: Thomas Y. Crowell, 1987.

Tebbel, John. *Turning the World Upside Down: Inside the American Revolution.* New York: Orion Books, 1993.

Wood, Gordon S. *The Creation of the American Republic, 1776–1787.* Chapel Hill: University of North Carolina Press, 1969.

Media Resources

Educational Media

The American Revolution. 300 minutes. 1994. A six–part series from Arts and Entertainment (A&E). Available from Zenger Media, 800-421-4246.

The American Revolution: Two Views. Queue Corp., 1994. CD-ROM available in both DOS and Macintosh that presents the British, as well as the American, perspective on the causes of the Revolution. Available from Zenger Media, 800-421-4246

Dawn of the American Revolution: A Lexington Family. 16 minutes. Learning Corporation of America. Videotape that reviews the causes of conflict as Lexington brothers gather on the battle green in April 1775. Available from Zenger Media, 800-421-4246.

Feature Films

Johnny Tremain. 80 minutes. Films, Inc./Walt Disney Home Video, 1957. Based on the Newbery Award-winning book by Esther Forbes. Available from Zenger Media, 800-421-4246.

1776. 148 minutes. RCA-Columbia Pictures Home Video, 1972. Re-creation of the Second Continental Congress in Philadelphia, featuring the leaders of American independence. Available from Zenger Media, 800-421-4246

UNIT 3

Andrew Jackson and the Removal of the Cherokee Nation

HISTORICAL BACKGROUND

Andrew Jackson was born in 1767 in the border area between North and South Carolina. His Scotch-Irish parents had emigrated to America from Ireland two years before his birth. At age 13, Jackson joined the Continental Army as a courier and, along with his two brothers, saw service throughout the Revolution. His treatment by the British as a prisoner of war caused Jackson to resent the British his entire life. Both his brothers died during the war.

After the Revolutionary War, Jackson taught school, but found this not to his liking. In 1784, he went to Salisbury, North Carolina, to study law. He was admitted to the bar in 1787 and began practicing law in Nashville, Tennessee. When Tennessee became the sixteenth state, Jackson was elected as the state's first representative to Congress. The next year he became a senator, but resigned after one session. It is thought that Jackson found the Senate too conservative and inactive for his taste, which had been formed by his frontier background. Jackson returned to Tennessee and served as a judge on the state supreme court.

In 1802, Jackson was elected major general of the Tennessee militia and later a major general in the United States military. He led several campaigns against Native Americans in the Creek War and later in the first Seminole War in Florida. He became a hero on the national level during the War of 1812, when he defeated the British at the Battle of New Orleans. It was during this war that he received his nickname, "Old Hickory," because of his toughness.

In 1824, Jackson ran for president. Although he won the popular vote, he did not have enough electoral votes, so the election was decided by the House of Representatives. The speaker of the house, Henry Clay, gave his support to John Quincy Adams, who saw Jackson as a "country bumpkin" incapable of governing the nation. Jackson lost the election. He never forgave either Clay or Adams, especially since Adams had accused Jackson and his wife, Rachel, of adultery. Jackson had married Rachel in 1791 while she was still legally married to her first husband. Although Jackson and his wife swore it was a legal misunderstanding and remarried when her divorce was finalized, gossip and rumors plagued them both throughout Jackson's political career. When Rachel died just weeks before Jackson's inauguration as president in 1828, he blamed her death on the stress caused by the vicious attacks on her morality during the campaign. Jackson's habit of becoming involved in duels also provided material for the press.

In 1828, Jackson became the seventh president of the United States. Despite his lack of support for states' rights, Jackson was supported by southerners. They saw him as an alternative to Adams, who clearly represented the northeast and had a disdain for the south and west. Jackson is sometimes referred to as the first populist president.

Although Jackson supported the power of the federal government over the states in issues such as the 1832 tariff, he did not insist on enforcing the laws regarding Native Americans. When the Supreme Court ruled that the

Critical Thinking Using
Primary Sources in U.S. History

State of Georgia had no jurisdiction over the Cherokees, Jackson made no effort to make Georgia abide by the decision. In 1838–39, Georgia forced the Cherokees to leave the state and march west. Federal troops under General Winfield Scott supervised the Cherokee removal, which was known to the Cherokees as the "Trail of Tears." This removal of the Cherokees took place during Martin Van Buren's presidency, but Jackson also believed that the tribes of the southeastern states should be moved to uninhabited lands west of the Mississippi. While Jackson was president, the Indian Removal Act of 1830 was passed. It offered Indians land in the west if they would evacuate their tribal lands in the east.

Despite poor health, Jackson lived to complete his presidency and even saw to it that his handpicked successor, Martin Van Buren, was elected to follow him. Jackson retired to his home near Nashville, where he died in 1845.

Key Questions About This Subject

- Jackson supported the power of the federal government over that of the states. Why, then, was his record different concerning the states and the removal of Native Americans?
- What were Jackson's arguments for the removal of Native Americans to uninhabited lands in the west?

- Why did he feel that removal would benefit the Indians themselves?
- How did the leaders of the native tribes respond to the proposal to remove the tribes for their own good?
- What do you feel is the real, yet unstated, reason for Indian removal?

Mock Trial

If you are going to hold a simulated trial, here are the charges against Andrew Jackson (the Defendant): Andrew Jackson, president of the United States, is charged with the forcible removal of Native Americans from their homelands and the deaths of many Native Americans as they were compelled to move to land west of the Mississippi.

DOCUMENTS

Document A

President Andrew Jackson's Case for the Removal Act: First Annual Message to Congress, December 8, 1830

(From the *Congressional Record*, 1830. As found in Louis Filler and Allen Guttmann, eds., *The Removal of the Cherokee Nation: Manifest Destiny or National Dishonor?* Boston: D.C. Heath, 1962.)

It gives me pleasure to announce to Congress that the benevolent policy of the Government, steadily pursued for nearly thirty years, in relation to the removal of the Indians beyond the white settlements is approaching to a happy consummation. Two important tribes have accepted the provision made for their removal at the last session of Congress, and it is believed that their example will induce the remaining tribes also to seek the same obvious advantages.

The consequences of a speedy removal will be important to the United States, individual States, and to the Indians themselves. The pecuniary advantages which it promises to the Government are the least of its recommendations. It puts an end to all possible danger of a collision between the authorities of the General and State Governments on account of the Indians. It will place a dense and civilized population in large tracts of country now occupied by a few savage hunters. By opening the whole territory between Tennessee on the north and Louisiana on the south to the settlement of the whites it will incalculably strengthen the southwestern frontier and render the adjacent States strong enough to repel future invasions without remote aid. It will relieve the whole State of Mississippi and the western part of Alabama of Indian occupancy, and enable those States to advance rapidly in population, wealth, and power. It will separate the Indians from immediate contact with settlements of whites; free them from the power of the States; enable them to pursue happiness in their own way and under their own rude institutions; will retard the progress of decay, which is lessening their numbers, and perhaps cause them gradually, under the protection of the Government and through the influence of good counsels, to cast off their savage habits and become an interesting, civilized, and Christian community. . . .

Towards the aborigines of the country no one can indulge a more friendly feeling than myself, or would go further in attempting to reclaim them from their wandering habits and make them a happy, prosperous people. . . .

Humanity has often wept over the fate of the aborigines of this country, and Philanthropy has been long busily employed in devising means to avert it, but its progress has never for a moment been arrested, and one by one have many powerful tribes disappeared from the earth. To follow to the tomb the last of his race and to tread on the graves of extinct nations excite melancholy reflections. But true philanthropy reconciles the mind to these vicissitudes as it does to the extinction of one generation to make room for another. In the monuments and fortresses of an unknown people, spread over the extensive regions of the West, we behold the memorials of a once powerful race, which was exterminated or has disappeared to make room for the existing savage tribes. Nor is there anything in this which, upon a comprehensive view of the general interests of the human race, is to be regretted. Philanthropy could not wish to see this continent restored to the conditions in which it was found by our forefathers. What good man would prefer a country covered with forests and ranged by a few thousand savages to our extensive Republic, studded with cities, towns, and prosperous farms, embellished with all the improvements which art can devise or industry execute, occupied by more than 12,000,000 happy people, and filled with all the blessings of liberty, civilization, and religion?

Document B

"Letter to the American People" from Choctaw Chief George W. Harkins

(As found in Jim Carnes, *Us and Them: A History of Intolerance in America.* Montgomery, AL: Southern Poverty Law Center, 1995, pp. 20–21.)

It is said that our present movements are our own voluntary acts—such is not the case. We found ourselves like a benighted stranger, following false guides, until he was surrounded on every side, with fire or water. The fire was certain destruction, and a feeble hope was left him of escaping by water. A distant view of the opposite shore encourage the hope; to remain would be inevitable annihilation. Who would hesitate, or who would say that his plunging into the water was his own voluntary act? Painful in the extreme is the mandate of our expulsion. We regret that it should proceed from the mouth of our professed friend, and for whom our blood was commingled with that of his bravest warriors, on the field of danger and death.

But such is the instability of professions. The man who said that he would plant a stake and draw a line around us, that never should be passed, was the first to say he could not guard that line, and drew up the stake and wiped out all traces of the line. I will not conceal from you my fears, that the present grounds may be removed. . . . Who of us can tell after witnessing what has already been done, what the next force may be. I ask you in the name of justice, for repose for myself and for my injured people. Let us alone—we will not harm you, we want rest. . . . As east of the Mississippi we have been friends, so west we will cherish the same feelings with additional fervour; and although we may be removed to the desert, still we shall look with fond regard upon those who have promised us their protection.

Friends, my attachment to my native land was strong—that cord is now broken; and we must go forth as wanderers in a strange land! . . . Let me intreat you to regard us with feelings of kindness, and when the hand of oppression is stretched against us, let me hope that a warning voice may be heard from every part of the U[nited] States, filling the mountains and valleys with echo, and say stop, you have no power, we are the sovereign people, and our red friends shall no more be disturbed.

David Crockett: From a Speech Before Congress, May 19, 1830

(From "Speeches on the Passage of the Bill for the Removal of the Indians." Boston: Perkins & Marvin, 1830, pp. 251–253. As found in Louis Filler and Allen Guttmann, ed., *Removal of the Cherokee Nation: Manifest Destiny or National Dishonor?* Boston: D.C. Heath, 1962, p. 39–41.)

Mr. Crockett said that, considering his very humble abilities, it might be expected that he should content himself with a silent vote; but, situated as he was, in relation to his colleagues, he felt it to be a duty to himself to explain the motives which governed him in the vote he should give on this bill. Gentlemen had already discussed the treaty-making power; and had done it much more ably than he could pretend to do. He should not therefore enter on that subject, but would merely make an explanation as to the reasons of his vote. He did not know whether a man (that is, a member of Congress) within 500 miles of his residence would give a similar vote; but he knew, at the same time, that he should give that vote with a clear conscience. He had his constituents to settle with, he was aware; and should like to please them as well as other gentlemen; but he had also a settlement to make at the bar of his God; and what his conscience dictated to be just and right he would do, be the consequences what they might. . . . He had always viewed the native Indian tribes of this country as sovereign people. He believed they had been recognized as such from the very foundation of this government, and the United States were bound by treaty to protect them; it was their duty to do so. And as to giving the money of the American people for the purpose of removing them in the manner proposed, he would not do it. He would that only for which he could answer to his God. . . .

Mr. C. [Crockett] said that four counties of his district bordered on the Chickasaw country. He knew many of their tribe and nothing should ever induce him to vote to drive them west of the Mississippi. He did not know what sort of a country it was in which they were to be settled. He would willingly appropriate money in order to send proper persons to examine the country. And when this had been done, and a fair and free treaty had been made with the tribes, if they were desirous of removing, he would vote an appropriation of any sum necessary; but till this had been done, he would not vote one cent. . . . Government had taken measures to purchase land from the Indians who had gone to Arkansas. If this bill should pass, the same plan would be carried further; they would send and buy them out, and put white men upon their land. . . . Now, if this was not oppression with a vengeance, he did not know what was. . . . He knew that Indians were unwilling to go: therefore he could not consent to place them in a situation where they would be obliged to go. He could not stand that. . . . He had been charged with not representing his constituents. If the fact was so, the error (said Mr. C.) is here (touching his head), not here (laying his hand upon his heart). He never had possessed wealth or education, but he had ever been animated by an independent spirit; and he trusted to prove it on the present occasion.

"Cherokee Editor Elias Boudinot Opposes Removal, 1828."

(As found in Albert L. Hurtado and Peter Iverson, eds., *Major Problems in American Indian History.* Lexington, MA: D.C. Heath, 1994, p. 210.)

. . . Our last Washington papers contain a debate which took place in the house of representatives, on the resolution, recommended by the Committee on Indian Affairs, published in the second Number of our paper. It appears that the advocates of this new system of civilizing the Indians are very strenuous in maintaining the novel opinion, that it is impossible to enlighten the Indians, surrounded as they are by the white population, and that they assuredly will become extinct, unless they are removed. It is a fact which we would not deny, that many tribes have perished away in consequence of white population, but we are yet to be convinced that this will always be the case, in spite of every measure taken to civilize them. We contend that suitable measures to a sufficient extent have never been employed. And how dare these men make an assertion without sufficient evidence? What proof have they that the system which they are now recommending, will succeed? Where have we an example in the whole history of man, of a Nation or tribe, removing in a body, from a land of civil and religious means, to a perfect wilderness, *in order to be civilized.* We are fearful these men are building castles in the air, whose fall will crush those poor Indians who may be blinded as to make the experiment. We are sorry to see that some of the advocates of this system speak so disrespectfully, if not contemptuously, of the present measures of improvement, now in successful operation among most of the Indians in the United States—the only measures too, which have been crowned with success, and bid fair to meliorate the condition of the Aborigines. . . .

Wilson Lumpkin: Speech Before Congress, May 17, 1830

(From Gales & Seaton, *Register of Debates in Congress*, Vol. VI, Part 2, pp. 1020–1023. As found in Louis Filler and Allen Guttmann, eds., *The Removal of the Cherokee Nation: Manifest Destiny or National Dishonor?* Boston: D.C. Heath, 1962, pp. 31–38.)

Amongst my earliest recollections are the walls of an old fort, which gave protection to the women and children from the tomahawk and scalping knife of the Indians. And let me inform you, that, while the Indians have receded thousands of miles before the civilized population in other sections of the Union, the frontier of Georgia has comparatively remained stationary. My present residence is not more than one day's travel from the place of the old fort to which I alluded. It is but part of a day's travel from my residence to the line of the Cherokee country. . . .

Sir, I blame not the Indians; I commiserate their case. I have considerable acquaintance with the Cherokees, and amongst them I have seen much to admire. To me, they are in many respects an interesting people. If the wicked influence of designing men, veiled in the garb of philanthropy and christian benevolence, should excite the Cherokees to a course that will end in their speedy destruction, I now call upon this Congress, and the whole American people, not to charge the Georgians with this sin; but let it be remembered that it is the fruit of cant and fanaticism, emanating from the land of steady habits, from the boasted progeny of pilgrims and puritans.

Sir, my State stands charged before this House, before the nation, and before the whole world, with cruelty and oppression towards the Indians. I deny the charge, and demand proof from those who made it. . . . No man living entertains kinder feelings to the Indians than Andrew Jackson. If any President of the United States has deserved the appellation of friend and father to the Indians, it is him who is now at the helm. . . . He not only is, but has been, their true friend and benefactor. . . .

The absolute rulers of the Cherokee country, like other men, love office, distinction, and power. They are enjoying great and peculiar benefits. They do not like the idea of becoming private citizens. It is with great reluctance they yield up their stewardship. They know they have not been faithful to the interest of the poor degraded Indians. They know the great mass of their people have been left to suffer in want and ignorance, whilst they have spent their substance in forming foreign alliance with an enthusiastic, selfish, money-loving people. . . . And if they join the western Cherokees, they cannot carry with them their present assumed sovereignty and rule. They will there find equals in many of their pioneer brethren. . . . George Guess [Sequoyah], and many others, are already there. Yes sir, these Cherokees are in the full enjoyment of all the blessings of their emigrating enterprise, and there is but one opinion among them as to their relative comfort and prospect of future blessings. All the various emigrants to the West so far agree as to authorize the assurance that no inducement could be offered to them strong enough to bring them back again.

The Cherokees and Creeks are charmed with their country, and to the many things which attach to their comfort in it. The New England farmers who have emigrated to the fertile valleys of the West, would as soon consent to return to the barren sand and sterile rocks of their native land, as a western Cherokee or Creek would return to the sepulchre of his forefathers. . . .

Resources

Bibliography

Carnes, Jim. *Us and Them: A History of Intolerance in America.* Montgomery, AL: Southern Poverty Law Center, 1995.

Filler, Louis, and Allen Guttmann, eds. *The Removal of the Cherokee Nation: Manifest Destiny or National Dishonor?* Boston: D.C. Heath and Company, 1962.

Hurtado, Albert L., and Peter Iverson, eds. *Major Problems in American Indian History.* Lexington, MA: D.C. Heath and Company, 1994.

Meyers, Madeleine, ed. *The Cherokee Nation: Life Before the Tears.* Lowell, MA: Discovery Enterprises, Ltd., 1994.

Osinski, Alice. *Andrew Jackson: Seventh President of the United States (Encyclopedia of Presidents).* Danbury, CT: Children's Book Press, 1987.

Remini, Robert Vincent. *The Legacy of Andrew Jackson: Essays on Democracy, Indian Removal, and Slavery.* Baton Rouge: Louisiana State University Press, 1990.

Remini, Robert Vincent. *Andrew Jackson and the Course of American Democracy, 1833–1845.* New York: Harper & Row, 1984.

Michael Paul Rogin. *Fathers and Children: Andrew Jackson and the Subjugation of the American Indian.* Piscataway, NJ: Transaction Publishers, 1975.

Schlesinger, Arthur M. *The Age of Jackson.* Boston: Little, Brown and Company, 1945.

Sherrow, Victoria. *Cherokee Nation v. Georgia: Native American Rights (Landmark Supreme Court Cases).* Springfield, NJ: Enslow Publishers, 1997.

Wilson, Wendy S., and Lloyd Thompson. *Native Americans: A Thematic Unit on Converging Cultures.* Portland, ME: J. Weston Walch, Publisher, 1997.

Media Resources

The Jackson Years: The New Americans and *The Jackson Years: Toward Civil War.* 27 minutes each. Learning Corporation of America. Available from Zenger Media, 800-421-4246.

How the West Was Lost. 350 minutes total, seven episodes. Discovery Channel, 1995. Details Indian removal and the Trail of Tears. Available from Zenger Media, 800-421-4246.

500 Nations. 49 minutes each part. Columbia House, 1994. Eight-part documentary series, with volume 6, titled *Removal,* presenting the removal of the southern tribes to the West. Available from Zenger Media, 800-421-4246.

HISTORICAL BACKGROUND

Lansford Warren Hastings was born in Mt. Vernon, Ohio, in 1819. As a young adult, he became a lawyer. In 1842, at the age of 23, he joined a group of emigrants in Kansas and headed west with them to Oregon. Pioneers who traveled to the west were known as "emigrants" because they were seen as moving outside of United States territory. Hastings arrived in the Willamette Valley in the Oregon Territory, but only stayed a short time. He then journeyed down the coast to Sutter's Fort in California, where he became convinced that this land had great potential for settlement. It is believed that Hastings had ambitions of setting up an independent California republic with himself as president or, should California become a state, that he would try to become governor.

In 1844, Hastings returned east. He published a book, *Emigrants' Guide to Oregon and California,* in Cincinnati in 1845. The book sold very well and the timing was perfect—many people were considering a move to the west. In the book, Hastings made reference to a shortcut to California, later known as the "Hastings Cutoff," which he believed would save valuable time on the journey. Hastings promoted the cutoff among the emigrants of the summer of 1846 as a way to get people to move to California instead of Oregon. A party of emigrants from Illinois, known as the Donner Party, decided to try the cutoff. With great difficulty, Hastings had succeeded in leading a group of 80 wagons to California using the cutoff. But the route proved to be a disaster for the Donner Party, which lost much time in crossing the mountains and the Salt Desert.

The Donner Party became so delayed that they missed the chance to cross the Sierras before the winter snows. They were stranded in the mountains by the most severe winter in the history of the area, which resulted in a great loss of life. Some of the survivors resorted to cannibalism in order to stay alive. The story of the tragedy of the Donner Party and the extraordinary relief efforts to get the stranded emigrants out of the mountains was widely publicized.

Hasting's guide and his cutoff were discredited because of the Donner Tragedy, and he ceased to lead emigrants to California. He settled down to practice law and was elected to the California state convention in 1849.

After the Civil War, Hastings went to South America and published an emigrant's guide to Brazil. Hastings died in 1870 while leading a group of colonists to Brazil.

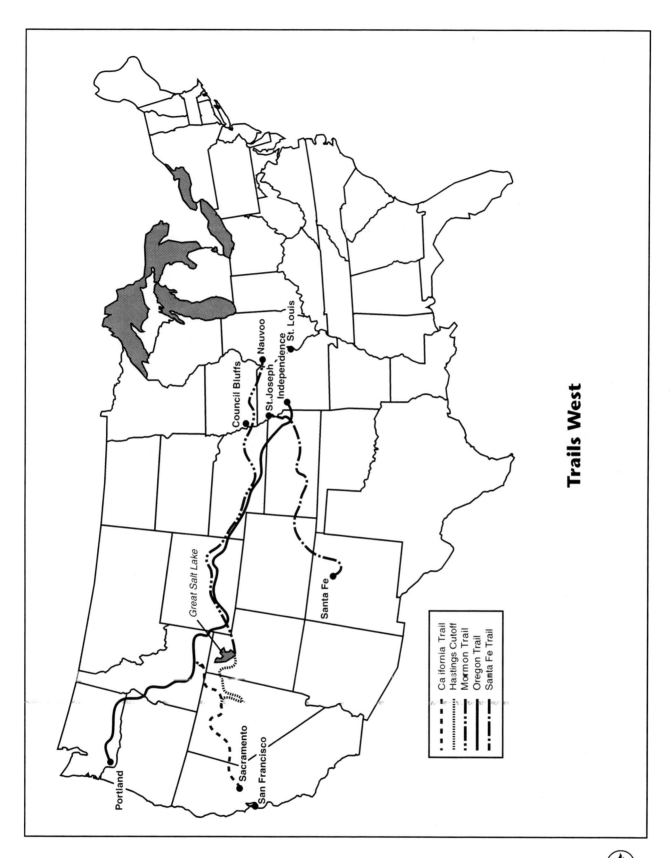

Trails West

Nauvoo

St. Louis

Independence

St. Joseph

Council Bluffs

Great Salt Lake

Santa Fe

Portland

Sacramento

San Francisco

California Trail
Hastings Cutoff
Mormon Trail
Oregon Trail
Santa Fe Trail

Critical Thinking Using
Primary Sources in U.S. History

Key Questions About This Subject

- What were Hastings' objectives in publishing his *Emigrants' Guide*?
- Why was he anxious to find a shortcut to California?
- Had any group ever used the Hastings Cutoff before the Donner Party?
- Why did the Donner Party decide to use the shortcut and leave the other group with whom they were traveling?

- Why did the tragedy of the Donner Party make such a mark on American history and subsequent journeys out west?
- Can one person really be blamed for the tragedy, or was it simply a combination of bad luck and bad judgment?

Mock Trial

If you are going to hold a simulated trial, here are the charges against Lansford W. Hastings (the Defendant): Lansford Warren Hastings, promoter of the territory known as California and writer of *Emigrants' Guide to Oregon and California*, is charged with negligent homicide in causing the deaths of 41 members of the Donner Party, emigrants to California in 1846, by advocating the use of a shortcut, subsequently known as the Hastings Cutoff, which had not been tried by emigrant wagons.

DOCUMENTS

Document A

Westward Routes

(From Lansford W. Hastings, *Emigrants' Guide to Oregon and California.* Cincinnati: G Concklin, 1945. Facsimile reprint, Bedford, MA: Applewood Books, 1994, pp. 134 and 137.)

We are necessarily driven to this conclusion, when we consider the vast extent of [this infant country's] plains and valleys, of unequalled fertility and exuberance; the extraordinary variety and abundance, of its productions, its unheard of uniformity, and salubrity of climate; in fine, its unexhausted and inexhaustible resources, as well as its increasing emigration, which is annually swelling its population from hundreds to thousands, and which is destined, at no distant day to revolutionize the whole commercial, political, and moral aspect of all that highly important and delightful country. . . . In a word, I will remark that in my opinion, there is no country, in the known world, possessing a soil so fertile and productive, with such varied and inexhaustible resources, and a climate of such mildness, uniformity and salubrity; nor is there a country, in my opinion, now known, which is so eminently calculated, by nature herself, in all respects, to promote the unbounded happiness and prosperity, of civilized and enlightened man. . . .

By recent explorations, however, a very good, and much more direct wagon way, has been found, about one hundred miles, southward from the great southern pass, which, it will be observed, lies principally through the northern part of California. The California route, from Fort Hall to the Sacramento river, lies through alternate plains, prairies and valleys, and over hills, amid lofty mountains; thence down the great valley of the Sacramento, to the bay of St. Francisco, a distance from Fort Hall, of nine hundred miles. The Indians are, in many places, very numerous; yet they are extremely timid, and entirely inoffensive. Wagons can be as readily taken from Fort Hall to the bay of St. Francisco, as they can, from the States to Fort Hall; and, in fact, the latter part of the route, is found much more eligible for a wagon way, than the former.

The most direct route, for the California emigrants, would be to leave the Oregon route, about two hundred miles east from Fort Hall; thence bearing west southwest, to the Salt lake; and thence continuing down to the bay of St. Francisco, by the route just described. The emigrants, up to this time, however, have traveled together, as far as Fort Hill, because of this being the only settlement, in that vicinity, at which they are enabled to procure horses, and provisions. The soda springs, however, will, undoubtedly be found to be the point at which the routes will most advantageously diverge, both in reference to directness, and to the obtaining of supplies; for there is no doubt, but that a town, of very considerable importance, will spring up, at that point, in a very few years. The entire distance by this route, from Independence, either to Oregon or California, is about twenty-one hundred miles; and the usual time required in performing the journey, to either of those countries, will be found to be about one hundred and twenty days, exclusive of delays; yet the great disadvantages, under which parties have, heretofore, labored, have caused them to occupy much more time, than that above stated, in performing the journey. It is a surprising fact, that upon this entire route, from the States, either to Oregon or California, there is not a stream that emigrants cross, but that is fordable, at the season of the year, at which they pass through those regions. A much better way, is generally found, the entire extent of this route, than can be found, in any portion of our western States, the same distance, especially from the States to California, by the route just described.

Letter

(Excerpts from a letter by Virginia Reed, May 16, 1847, as found in George R. Stewart, *Ordeal by Hunger*. Lincoln: University of Nebraska Press, 1986. Original spelling and grammar have not been corrected.)

My Dear Cousin,

I take this opportunity to write to you to let you now that we are all Well at present and hope this letter may find you all well to My Dear Cousin I am going to write to you about our trubels geting to California. We had good luck we come to big Sandy thare we lost our best yoak of oxens we come to Brigers Fort & we lost another ox we sold some of our provisions & baut a yoax of Cows and oxen and thay pursuaded us to take Hastings cutof over the salt plain thay said it saved 3 Hundred miles. we went that road & we had to go through a long drive of 40 miles With out water Hastings said it was 40 but i think 80 miles. . . . We had to walk all the time we was a travling up the truckee river. . . . it was rain g then in the Vallies and snowing on the mountains so we went on that way 3 or 4 days till we come to the big mountain or the California Mountain the snow then was about 3 feet deep thare was some wagons thare thay said thay had atempted to croos and could not. well we thought we would try it so we started and thay started again with those wagons the snow was then up to the mules side the farther we went up the deeper the snow got so the wagons could not go. . . . we stoped thare the 4 th of November and staid till March and what we had to eat i cant hardley tell you. . . . we had nothing to eat but ox hides o Mary I would cry and wish I had what you all wasted Eliza had to go to Mrs. Graves cabin & we staid at Mr. Breen thay had meat all the time. & we had to kill littel cash the dog & eat him we ate his entrails and feet & hide & evry thing about him o my Dear Cousin you dont now what trubel is yet. Many a time we had on the last thing a cooking and did not now wher the next would come from but there was awl weis some way provided there was 15 in the cabon we was in and half of us had to lay a bed all the time thare was 10 starved to death then we was hadly abel to walk we lived on little cash a week and after Mr. Breen would cook his meat we would take the bones and boil them 3 or 4 days at a time. . . . thare was but [2] familes that all of them got [through] we was one O Mary I have not rote you half of the truble we have had but I have rote you anuf to let you now that you dont now what truble is but thank god we have all got throw and the onely family that did not eat human flesh we have left everything but i dont cair for that we have got throw with our lives but Dont let this letter dish[e]a[r]ten anybody never take no cutofs and hury along as fast as you can.

Critical Thinking Using
Primary Sources in U.S. History

Narrative

(Excerpts from Jacob Wright Harlan, *California, '46 to '88.* San Francisco: Bancroft, 1988. As found in Kristin Johnson, ed., *"Unfortunate Emigrants": Narratives of the Donner Party.* Logan: Utah State University Press, 1996, pp. 233–261.)

> **Note:** Jacob Wright Harlan was a member of a party of emigrants known as the Harlan-Young Party. They took the Hastings Cutoff just ahead of the Donner Party, but were able to make it to California before the snows hit the Sierras. There is one glaring error in this report. Harlan reported that the Donner Party traveled with the Harlan-Young Party as far as Weber River where they, according to Harlan, turned back. The Donner emigrants left several days after the Harlan-Young Party and at the Weber River took a new route that had never been traveled.

From Laramie we kept on to Fort Bridger, where we halted for three days. Here we met a man named L. W. Hastings, who had written the book which I have mentioned. He had just come from California and professed to know all about the proper way to get there. He got all the emigrants together, and recommended that we leave the old trail and make a cut off from Bridger to pass round the south end of the Salt Lake, and strike the Humboldt river one hundred and fifty miles above its sink. He said we would thus save three hundred miles of travel, it being that much nearer than the way by Fort Hall. There was a difference of opinion among our chief men. Governor Boggs and his company, our captain, Judge Moran, and some others were in favor of the Fort Hall route, but my uncle and old man Pyle, and James F. Reid [Reed], and George Donner were in favor of the cutoff recommended by Hastings. . . .

Our journey from Fort Bridger to Salt Lake was both difficult and disagreeable, especially when we had to travel through the sage-brush and grease-wood. When we had come to within a half mile of the lake we halted at "Weber cañon," a pass which for about a half mile seemed impracticable. Our four head men held a council. Reid and Donner declared it to be impossible for us to get through. My uncle and old man Pyle felt sure that we could; so there was a split. Reid and Donner turned, and trailed back for three days, and then crossed the mountains. We worked six days building a road, and got through on the seventh day. This put Reid and Donner ten days behind us. If they had helped us we would have got through on the fourth day. . . .

After having passed the desert, we found it necessary to rest our animals for three days, they were so exhausted and spirit-broken. On arriving at the Humboldt river we found that Governor Boggs' party was some seventy miles in advance of us, the Fort Hall route being the better after all. . . .

In dismissing this matter of the "starved camp" tragedy, I cannot but again advert to the fact that if Reid and Donner had stayed with Mr. Pyle and my uncle and helped us to make the road through the Weber cañon, they would have got through in safety, and both they and we, by arriving at the mountains so many days earlier, would have escaped many other troubles which afflicted us. Hastings was not to blame in this. He told Reid and Donner that he did not know the route which they wished to take, having never been over it. The blunder of all of us lay in our leaving the Fort Hall road, which was a well known and an easier route, and this is an illustration of the truth of the adage,

> "While you have a highway
> never take a bye way,
> E'en tho' it be a nigh way."

Narrrative

(Excerpt from H.A. Wise, *Los Gringos, or, An Inside View of Mexico and California, with Wanderings in Peru, Chili, and Polynesia.* New York: Baker and Schribner, 1850. As found in Kristin Johnson, ed., *"Unfortunate Emigrants": Narratives of the Donner Party.* Logan: Utah State University Press, 1996, pp. 134–135.)

Previous to our arrival in the waters of San Francisco, a frightful incident transpired amidst the California mountains, which goes far to surpass any event of the kind heard or seen. . . . It relates to a party of emigrants, whose shocking inhuman cannibalisms and sufferings exceeded all belief. The news first reached us in Monterey, and also that a party had been despatched to succor them. From an officer of the navy in charge of the expedition [Woodworth], and from one of the survivors, a Spanish boy, named Baptiste, I learned the following particulars: The number of emigrants were originally eighty; through a culpable combination of ignorance and folly, they loitered many weeks on the route, when, upon gaining the sierra, the snows set in, the trails became blocked up and impassable, and they were obliged to encamp for the winter; their provisions were shortly exhausted, their cattle were devoured to the last horse's hide, hunger came upon them, gaunt and terrible, starvation at last—men, women and children starved to death, and were eaten by their fellows— insanity followed. When relief arrived, the survivors were found rolling in filth, parents eating their own offspring, denizens of different cabins exchanging limbs and meat—little children tearing and devouring the livers and hearts of the dead, and a general apathy and mania pervaded all alike. . . . One Dutchman actually ate a full-grown body in thirty-six hours! another boiled and devoured a girl nine years old, in a single night. The women held on to life with greater tenacity than the men—in fact, the first intelligence was brought to Sutter's fort, on the Sacramento by two young girls. . . .There were thirty survivors, and a number of them without feet, either frozen or burnt off, who were placed under the care of our surgeons on shore. . . . The cause of all this suffering was mainly attributable to the unmeaning delay and indolence attending their early progress on the route, but with every advantage in favor of emigration, the journey in itself must be attended with immense privation and toil. The mere fact, that by the upper route there is one vast desert to be travelled over, many hundred miles in width, affording very little vegetation or sustenance, and to crown the difficulty, terminated by the rugged chain of Californian mountains, is almost sufficient in itself to deter many a good man and strong, from exposing his life and property, for an unknown home on the shores of the Pacific.

Narrrative

(Excerpt from J. Quinn Thornton, *Oregon and California in 1848*, two vols. New York: Harper & Bros., 1949. As found in Kristin Johnson, ed., *"Unfortunate Emigrants": Narratives of the Donner Party.* Logan: Utah State University Press, 1996, pp. 23–24.)

> **Note:** Jessy Quinn Thornton emigrated to Oregon in 1846. His party traveled with the Donner Party until they split off to try the Hastings Cutoff and Thornton's party continued via Fort Hall to Oregon. Thornton's group did take the new Applegate Cutoff to Oregon and suffered such hardship that Thornton later disputed bitterly with Jesse Applegate and David Goff, the promoters of this new trail.

Upon my arrival at the town of San Francisco [on November 10, 1847], I had the pleasure of receiving the friendly salutation and cordial greetings of many who had been my traveling companions in 1846. We had all commenced our journey together from the Wokaruska Creek, west of the frontier settlements of Missouri, with my valued friend Col. Russell for our leader. In the divisions and subdivisions of the company which subsequently occurred, at the times and places noted in my journal, we were separated. Our respective companies, however, often traveled near to each other, and not unfrequently we encamped at the same grass and water. The reader, by turning back to my journal entries, under the dates of July 21 and 22 [19 and 20], 1846, will see that these California emigrants, at that time, determined upon following Lansford W. Hastings, upon a "cut-off" into California. This man had left California, and proceeded as far as the eastern side of the Rocky Mountains, and encamped at a place where the Sweet Water breaks through a cañon, at the point where the emigrants leave that river to enter the South Pass. He had come out for the purpose of inducing the emigrants to follow him through a "cut-off" into California. After meeting some of the advanced companies, and sending forward a messenger with a letter to those in the rear, informing them that he had explored a new and much better road into California than the old one, he returned to Fort Bridger, where he stated that he would remain until the California and Oregon emigrants should come up, when he would give a more particular description of his "cut-off."

The emigrants having all in time arrived at that place, Hastings assured them in the most solemn manner that the road over which he proposed to conduct them, was much nearer and better than the one via Fort Hall. He stated that there was an abundant supply of wood, water, and grass upon the whole line of the road, except one dry drive of thirty-five miles, or of forty at most; that they would have no difficult cañons to pass, and that the road was generally smooth, level, and hard.

Upon meeting in California many of those who survived the dangers of that disastrous cut-off, some of them expressed a wish that I would embody the facts, and publish them to the world in connection with my own journal, as constituting an important part of the history of the journey of the emigration of that year to the Pacific coast.

Critical Thinking Using
Primary Sources in U.S. History

Resources

Bibliography

Bryant, Edwin. *What I Saw in California*. 1848. Reprint. Lincoln: University of Nebraska Press, 1985.

DeLafosse, Peter H., ed. *Trailing the Pioneers: A Guide to Utah's Emigrant Trails, 1829–1869*. Logan: Utah State University Press/Utah Crossroads, California-Oregon Trails Association, 1994.

DeVoto, Bernard. *Year of Decision, 1846*. Boston: Houghton Mifflin, 1943.

Johnson, Kristin, ed. *"Unfortunate Emigrants": Narratives of the Donner Party*. Logan: Utah State University Press, 1996. This book contains a very comprehensive bibliography about the Donner Party.

Kelly, Charles. *Salt Desert Trails: A History of the Hastings Cutoff and Other Early Trails Which Crossed the Great Salt Desert Seeking a Shorter Route to California*. Originally printed in 1930. Reprinted and edited by Peter DeLafosse, Hastings Cutoff Sesquicentennial Edition. Salt Lake City: Western Epics, 1996.

King, Joseph A. *Winter of Entrapment: A New Look at the Donner Party*. Revised edition. Walnut Creek: K & K, 1994.

McGlashan, C.F. *History of the Donner Party: A Tragedy of the Sierra*. Stanford: Stanford University Press, 1947.

Morgan, Dale L. *Overland in 1846: Diaries and Letters of the California-Oregon Trail*, two vols. Lincoln: University of Nebraska Press, 1993.

Stewart, George R. *Ordeal by Hunger: The Story of the Donner Party*. New edition. Lincoln: University of Nebraska Press, 1986.

Unruh, John D., Jr. *The Plains Across: The Overland Emigrants and the Trans-Mississippi West, 1840–60*. Chicago: University of Illinois Press, 1979.

Media Resources

The Donner Party. 90 minutes. Ric Burns documentary, with lesson plans and outline available. Available from PBS Video, 800-344-3337.

The West. 8 hours. Ken Burns presents a film by Stephen Ives, with lesson plans available. Available from PBS Video, 800-344-3337.

UNIT 5
Harriet Tubman and the Underground Railroad

Harriet Ross Tubman (her given name was Araminta Ross, but her owner called her Harriet) was born around 1820 (the exact date is uncertain), on a plantation in Maryland. She was born a slave and grew up working as a servant on the plantation. When Tubman was 13, she interfered with an attempt to apprehend a fleeing slave. Her master or an overseer hit her on the forehead with a lead weight, fracturing her skull and leaving her suffering from dizzy spells and blackouts for the rest of her life. Tubman married a freed slave, but he objected to her desire to escape. In 1849, Tubman decided to escape on her own.

Tubman fled northward (as had thousands of others) with the help of the Underground Railroad, an organization dedicated to helping slaves escape from the southern states through a network of safe houses, transporters, and guides. Working in Philadelphia as a cook and a servant, Tubman began to assist the Underground Railroad. Returning to Maryland to free her relatives, she became a "conductor," facing the double peril of being an escaped slave herself and engaging in this "illegal" activity. In all, she made some 19 trips into slave-owning states of the South, rescuing some 300 men, women, and children before the Civil War. In 1850, the year in which she began her rescue missions, Congress passed a new fugitive slave law, which made it much more difficult for escaped slaves to live in the northern states. As a result, the railroad began running escaped slaves to Canada, and Tubman moved to Ontario. By 1857, she had rescued her entire family and moved to New York, where she had bought land. There she met many abolitionists, including John Brown, whom she assisted in planning the raid on Harper's Ferry.

During the Civil War, Tubman worked for the Union as a nurse and as a spy behind Confederate lines. After the war she crusaded for various causes, mostly to help the newly freed slaves. Tubman died in March of 1913. She is emblematic of the central role played by free African Americans in aiding fugitive bondspeople and, through the Vigilance Committees they formed in northern cities, acting to protect free African Americans in jeopardy from fugitive slave hunters.

Key Questions About This Subject

- How did the newly organized United States of America deal with the contentious issue of slavery?
- How did those opposed to slavery on moral or religious grounds view the institution of slavery? Did they feel that they were morally bound to obey the laws and court decisions as they enforced the rights of slaveholders?

- In what forms of civil disobedience did abolitionists engage?
- Did African Americans participate in these activities, and at what risk to themselves and their families?
- In what ways did these activities lead to the Civil War?

Mock Trial

If you are going to hold a simulated trial, here are the charges against Harriet Tubman (the Defendant): Harriet Tubman, an escaped slave, is accused of violating various state laws and the Fugitive Slave Law of 1793 by escaping north in 1849. She is also accused of violating both the 1793 and 1850 laws in organizing and participating in the escape of numerous slaves from the south. By establishing the routes for escape, and by inciting others to escape, she is guilty of participating in a conspiracy to undermine constitutional government and state sovereignty in the United States.

DOCUMENTS

Document A

United States Constitution (Excerpts)

Preamble

We the People of the United States, in Order to form a more perfect Union, establish Justice, insure domestic Tranquility, provide for the common defence, promote the general Welfare, and secure the Blessings of Liberty to ourselves and our Posterity, do ordain and establish this Constitution for the United States of America.

Article I, Section 2

. . . Representatives and direct Taxes shall be apportioned among the several States which may be included within this Union, according to their respective Numbers, which shall be determined by adding to the whole Number of free Persons, including those bound to Service for a Term of Years, and excluding Indians not taxed, three fifths of all other Persons. The actual

Enumeration shall be made within three Years after the first Meeting of the Congress of the United States, and within every subsequent Term of ten Years, in such Manner as they shall by Law direct. . . .

Article I, Section 9

The Migration or Importation of such Persons as any of the States now existing shall think proper to admit, shall not be prohibited by the Congress prior to the Year one thousand eight hundred and eight, but a Tax or duty may be imposed on such Importation, not exceeding ten dollars for each Person. . . .

Article IV, Section 2

. . . No Person held to Service or Labour in one State, under the Laws thereof, escaping into another, shall, in Consequence of any Law or Regulation therein, be discharged from such Service or Labour, but shall be delivered up on Claim of the Party to whom such Service or Labour may be due.

Document B

Uncle Tom's Cabin (Extract)

(From Harriet Beecher Stowe's novel *Uncle Tom's Cabin; or, Life Among the Lowly*, 1852.)

One morning, when the hands were mustered for the field, Tom noticed with surprise a new-comer among them, whose appearance excited his attention. It was a woman, tall and slenderly formed, with remarkably delicate hands and feet, and dressed in neat and respectable garments. By the appearance of her face, she might have been between thirty-five and forty; and it was a face that, once seen, could never be forgotten—one of those that at a glance seem to convey to us an idea of a wild, painful, and romantic history. . . . There was a fierce pride and defiance in every line of her face, in every curve of the flexible lip, in every motion of her body; but in her eye was a deep, settled night of anguish—an expression so hopeless and un-changing as to contrast fearfully with the scorn and pride expressed by her whole demeanour.

Where she came from, or who she was, Tom did not know. The first he did know, she was walking by his side, erect, and proud, in the dim grey of the dawn. To the gang, however, she was known; for there was much looking and turning of heads, and a smothered yet apparent exultation among the miserable, ragged, half-starved creatures by whom she was surrounded.

"Got to come to it at last—glad of it!" said one.
"He! he! he!" said another. "You will know how good it is, misse!"
"We'll see her work!"
"Wonder if she'll get a cutting-up at night, like the rest of us!"
"I'll be glad to see her down for a flogging. I'll be bound!" said another.

The woman took no notice of these taunts, but walked on with the same expression of angry scorn as if she heard nothing. . . .

Tom was soon busy at his work; but, as the woman was at no great distance from him, he often glanced an eye to her at her work. He saw at a glance that a native adroitness and handiness made the task to her an easier one than it proved to many. She picked very fast and very clean, and with an air of scorn, as if she despised both the work and the disgrace and humiliation of the circumstances in which she was placed.

In the course of the day Tom was working with the mulatto woman who had been bought in the same lot with himself. She was evidently in a condition of great suffering, and Tom often heard her praying, as she wavered and trembled, and seemed about to fall down. Tom silently, as he came near to her, transferred several handfuls of cotton from his own sack to hers.

"Oh, don't, don't!" said the woman, looking surprised; "it'll get you in trouble."

Just then Sambo came up. He seemed to have a special spite against this woman, and, flourishing his whip, said, in brutal, guttural tones, "What dis yer, Luce—foolin' a'?" and, with a word, kicking the woman with his heavy cowhide shoe, he struck Tom across the face with his whip.

Tom silently resumed his task; but the woman, before at the last point of exhaustion fainted.

"I'll bring her to!" said the driver, with a brutal grin. "I'll give her something better than camphire!" and, taking a pin from his coat-sleeve, he buried it to the head in her flesh. The woman groaned and half rose. "Get up, you beast, and work, will yer, or I'll show you a trick more!"

The woman seemed stimulated for a few moments to an unnatural strength, and worked with desperate eagerness.

"See that, you keep to dat, ar. . . .," said the man, "or yer'll wish yer's dead to-night, I reckin!"

"That I do now!" Tom heard her say; and again he heard her say, "O Lord, how long? O Lord, why don't you help us?"

At the risk of all that he might suffer, Tom came forward again and put all the cotton in his sack into the woman's.

"Oh, you musn't; you dunno what they'll do to ye!" said the woman.

"I can b'ar it," said Tom, "better'n you;" and he was at his place again. It passed in a moment.

Suddenly the stranger woman whom we have described, and who had, in the course of her work, come near enough to hear Tom's last words, raised her heavy black eyes and fixed them for a second on him; then, taking a quantity of cotton from her basket, she placed it in his.

"You know nothing about this place," she said, "or you wouldn't have done that. When you've been here a month, you'll be done helping anybody; you'll find it hard enough to take care of your own skin."

The Fugitive Slave Law, February 12, 1793 (Extract)

An Act respecting fugitives from justice, and persons escaping from the service of their masters.
. . . Section 3. *And be it also enacted*, That when a person held to labor in any of the United States, or in either of the Territories on the Northwest or South of the river Ohio, under the laws thereof, shall escape into any other of the said States or Territory, the person to whom such labor or service may be due, his agent or attorney, is hereby empowered to seize or arrest such fugitive from labor, and to take him or her before any Judge of the Circuit or District Courts . . . or before any magistrate of a county, city, or town corporate, wherein such seizure or arrest shall be made, and upon proof to the satisfaction of such Judge or magistrate of any such State or Territory, that the person so seized or arrested, doth, under the laws of the State or Territory, from which he or she fled, owe service or labor to the person claiming him or her, it shall be the duty of such Judge or magistrate to give a certificate thereof to such claimant, his agent, or attorney, which shall be sufficient warrant for removing the said fugitive from labor to the State or Territory from which he or she fled.
　　Section 4. *And be further enacted*, That any person who shall knowingly and willingly obstruct or hinder such claimant, his agent or attorney, in so seizing or arresting such fugitive from labor, or shall rescue such fugitive from such claimant, his agent or attorney, when so arrested pursuant to the authority herein given or declared; or shall harbor or conceal such person after notice that he or she was a fugitive from labor, as aforesaid, shall for either of the said offences, forfeit and pay the sum of five hundred dollars. Which penalty may be recovered by and for the benefit of such claimant, by action of debt, in any Court proper to try the same, saving moreover to the person claiming such labor or service his right of action for or on account of the said injuries or either of them.

Fugitive Slave Act, September 18, 1850

(*U.S. Statutes at Large*, Vol. IX, p. 462 ff.)

　　. . . Section 5. That it shall be the duty of all marshals and deputy marshals to obey and execute all warrants and precepts issued under the provisions of this act, when to them directed; and should any marshal or deputy marshal refuse to receive such warrant, or other process, when tendered, or to use all proper means diligently to execute the same, he shall, on conviction thereof, be fined in the sum of one thousand dollars, to the use of such claimant . . . and after arrest of such fugitive, by such marshal or his deputy, or whilst at any time in his custody under the provisions of this act, should such fugitive escape, whether with or without the assent of such marshal or his deputy, such marshal shall be liable, on his official bond, to be prosecuted for the benefit of such claimant, for the full value of the service or labor of said fugitive in the State, Territory, or District whence he escaped: and the better to enable the said commissioners, when thus appointed, to execute their duties faithfully and efficiently, in conformity with the requirements of the Constitution of the United States and of this act, they are hereby authorized and empowered, within their counties respectively, to appoint, . . . any one or more suitable persons, from time to time, to execute all such warrants and other process as may be issued by them in the lawful performance of their respective duties. . . .

Section 6. That when a person held to service or labor in any State or Territory of the United States, has heretofore or shall hereafter escape into another State or Territory of the United States, the person or persons to whom such service or labor may be due, . . . may pursue and reclaim such fugitive person, either by procuring a warrant from some one of the courts, judges, or commissioners aforesaid, of the proper circuit, district, or county, for the apprehension of such fugitive from service or labor, or by seizing and arresting such fugitive, where the same can be done without process, and by taking, or causing such person to be taken, forthwith before such court, judge, or commissioner, whose duty it shall be to hear and determine the case of such claimant in a summary manner; and upon satisfactory proof being made, . . . to use such reasonable force and restraint as may be necessary, under the circumstances of the case, to take and remove such fugitive person back to the State or Territory whence he or she may have escaped as aforesaid. In no trial or hearing under this act shall the testimony of such alleged fugitive be admitted in evidence. . . .

Section 7. That any persons who shall knowingly and willingly obstruct, hinder, or prevent such claimant, his agent, or attorney, or any person or persons lawfully assisting him, her, or them, from arresting such a fugitive from service or labor . . . or shall rescue, or attempt to rescue, such fugitive from service or labor, from the custody of such claimant, . . . or shall harbor or conceal such fugitive, so as to prevent the discovery and arrest of such person, after notice or knowledge of the fact that such person was a fugitive from service or labor, . . . shall, for either of said offences, be subject to a fine not exceeding one thousand dollars, and imprisonment not exceeding six months . . . and shall moreover forfeit and pay, by way of civil damages to the party injured by such illegal conduct, the sum of one thousand dollars, for each fugitive so lost as aforesaid.

Document E

Extract from the Opinion of U.S. Supreme Court Chief Justice Roger Taney for the Court

(In *Scott v. Sanford*, 19 How. [60 U.S.] 393, by a vote of 7 to 2, popularly known as the "Dred Scott" decision, 1857.)

It is difficult at this day to realize the state of public opinion in relation to that unfortunate race, which prevailed in the civilized and enlightened portions of the world at the time of the Declaration of Independence, and when the Constitution of the United States was framed and adopted. But the public history of every European nation displays it, in a manner too plain to be mistaken.

They had for more than a century before been regarded as beings of an inferior order; and altogether unfit to associate with the white race, either in social or political relations; and so far inferior, that they had no rights which the white man was bound to respect; and that the negro might justly and lawfully be reduced to slavery for his benefit. . . . This opinion was at that time fixed and universal in the civilized portion of the white race. It was regarded as an axiom in morals as well as in politics, which no one thought of disputing, or supposed to be open to dispute; and men in every grade and position in society daily and habitually acted upon it in their private pursuits, as well as in matters of public concern, without doubting for a moment the correctness of this opinion.

©2000 J. Weston Walch, Publisher   38   *Critical Thinking Using Primary Sources in U.S. History*

Henry Box Brown Story

(From William Still, *The Underground Railroad*. Philadelphia: People's Publishing House Co., 1872, pp. 81–85.)

Although the name of Henry Box Brown has been echoed over the land for a number of years, and the simple facts connected with his marvelous escape from slavery in a box published widely through the medium of anti-slavery papers, nevertheless it is not unreasonable to suppose that very little is generally known in relation to this case.

Briefly, the facts are these, which doubtless have never before been fully published—

Brown was a man of invention as well as a hero. In point of interest, however, his case is not more remarkable than many others. Indeed, neither before nor after escaping did he suffer one-half what many others have experienced.

He was decidedly an unhappy piece of property in the city of Richmond, Va. In the condition of a slave he felt that it would be impossible for him to remain. Full well did he know, however, that it was no holiday task to escape the vigilance of Virginia slave-hunters, or the wrath of an enraged master for committing the unpardonable sin of attempting to escape to a land of liberty. So Brown counted well the cost before venturing upon this hazardous undertaking. Ordinary modes of travel he concluded might prove disastrous to his hopes; he, therefore, hit upon a new invention altogether, which was to have himself boxed up and forwarded to Philadelphia direct by express. The size of the box and how it was to be made to fit him most comfortably, was of his own ordering. Two feet eight inches deep, two feet wide, and three feet long were the exact dimensions of the box, lined with baize.[1] His resources with regard to food and water consisted of the following: One bladder of water and a few small biscuits. His mechanical implement to meet the death-struggle for fresh air, all told, was one large gimlet.[2] Satisfied that it would be far better to peril his life for freedom in this way than to remain under the galling yoke of Slavery, he entered his box, which was safely nailed up and hooped with five hickory hoops, and was then addressed by his next friend, James A. Smith, a shoe dealer, to Wm. H. Johnson, Arch street, Philadelphia, marked, "This side up with care." In this condition he was sent to Adams' Express office in a dray, and thence by overland express to Philadelphia. It was twenty-six hours from the time he left Richmond until his arrival in the City of Brotherly Love. The notice, "This side up, &c.," did not avail with the different expressmen, who hesitated not to handle the box in the usual rough manner common to this class of men. For a while they actually had the box upside down, and had him on his head for miles. A few days before he was expected, certain intimation was conveyed to a member of the Vigilance Committee that a box might be expected by the three o'clock morning train from the South, which might contain a man. . . .

Next morning, according to arrangement, the box was at the Anti-Slavery office in due time. The witnesses present to behold the resurrection were J.M. McKim, Professor C.D. Cleveland, Lewis Thompson, and the writer. . . .

All was quiet. The door had been safely locked. The proceedings commenced. Mr. McKim rapped quietly on the lid of the box and called out, "All right!" Instantly came the answer from within, "All right, sir!"

The witnesses will never forget that moment. Saw and hatchet quickly had the five hickory hoops cut and the lid off, and the marvellous resurrection of Brown ensued. Rising up in his box, he reached out his hand, saying, "How do you do, gentlemen?" The little assemblage hardly knew what to think or do at the moment. He was about as wet as if he had come up out of the Delaware. Very soon he remarked that, before leaving Richmond he had selected for his arrival-hymn (if he lived) the Psalm beginning with these words: *"I waited patiently for the Lord, and He heard my prayer."* And most touchingly did he sing the psalm, much to his own relief, as well as to the delight of his small audience.

[1]A coarse woolen or cotton napped fabric
[2]Tool for boring holes

40   *Critical Thinking Using Primary Sources in U.S. History*

Resources

Bibliography

Bennett, Lerone, Jr. "Free for Christmas." *Ebony,* December 1984, pp. 52–58.

Bradford, Sarah H. *Harriet Tubman: The Moses of Her People,* Gloucester, MA: P. Smith, 1981.

Bradford, Sarah H. *Scenes in the Life of Harriet Tubman.* Gloucester, MA: P. Smith, 1981.

Cover, Robert M. *Justice Accused: Antislavery and the Judicial Process.* New Haven, CT: Yale University Press, 1975, 1990.

Encyclopedia of African American Culture and History. New York: Simon and Schuster, 1996.

Freedman, Lawrence J. *Gregarious Saints: Self and Community in American Abolitionism.* New York: Cambridge University Press, 1982.

Harding, Vincent. *There Is a River: The Black Struggle for Freedom in America.* New York: Harcourt Brace Jovanovich, 1981.

Jones, Jacqueline. *Labor of Love, Labor of Sorrow: Black Women, Work and the Family from Slavery to the Present.* New York: Basic Books, 1985.

Litwak, Leon. *North of Slavery: The Negro in the Free States, 1790–1860.* Chicago: University of Chicago Press, 1961.

Potter, David M., and Don E. Fehrenbacher. *The Impending Crisis, 1848–1861.* New York: Harper & Row, 1976.

Sterling, Dorothy. *Freedom Train: The Story of Harriet Tubman.* Garden City, NY: Doubleday, 1954.

Media Resources

Documentaries

Africans in America. 90 minutes each part. PBS, 1998. A four-part series about slavery and race in the settlement of North America and the pre–Civil War era of U.S. history. It raises fundamental questions about the nature of our constitutional system's founding. The third and fourth parts, *Brotherly Love: 1787–1834* and *Judgment Day: 1831–1861*, deal with the issues of fugitive slaves. Series or individual parts available from PBS Video, 800-344-3337.

Flight to Freedom: The Underground Railroad. 109 minutes. Available from Films for Humanities and Sciences, 800-257-5126.

Frederick Douglass: When the Lion Wrote History. 90 minutes. PBS, 1994. Narrated by Alfre Woodward, this is a portrait of the escaped slave, abolitionist, journalist, and diplomat. Available from PBS Video, 800-344-3337, or Filmic Archives, 800-366-1920.

Harriet Tubman, Antislavery Activist. Bala Cynwyd, PA: Schlessinger Video Productions, 1992.

The History of Slavery in the United States. 82 minutes. Plymouth, MN: Simitar Entertainment, 1993. A set of two videocassettes.

Roots of Resistance—A Story of the Underground Railroad. Part of the PBS series *The American Experience.* Narrated by Ruby Dee, the program uses interviews with descendants of both slaves and slave owners, slave narratives, and other documents, photographs, location footage, dramatic re-creations, and music to show how slaves struggled to achieve their freedom. The program contains briefly shown photographs of nude slaves and some racist language. Available from PBS Video, 800-344-3337, or Zenger Media, 800-421-4246.

Feature Films

Presenting Mr. Frederick Douglass: The Lesson of the Hour. 60 minutes. A film version of Fred Morsell's dramatic theater piece in which he recreates Douglass' speech on slavery and human rights. Available from Films for the Humanities and Sciences, 800-257-5126.

Profiles in Courage: Frederick Douglass. 50 minutes. 1964. An episode in the John F. Kennedy book inspired this dramatization about Douglass' fight against the Fugitive Slave Act. Douglass is played by Robert Hooks, who also stars in *A Woman Called Moses.* The pre–Civil War struggle over slavery is also presented in two other dramatizations in this series, *Profiles in Courage: Thomas Hart Benton* and *Profiles in Courage: Daniel Webster.* All available from Zenger Media, 800-421-4246.

Race to Freedom: The Story of the Underground Railroad. 90 minutes. Xenon, 1994. A made-for-cable film dramatizing the story of four fugitive slaves who travel from North Carolina to Canada in 1850. Available from Teacher's Video Company, 800-262-8837.

Uncle Tom's Cabin. Three versions of Harriet Beecher Stowe's novel exist on film. The silent version (54 minutes, 1914) and a made-for-TV version (110 minutes, 1987) are available from Facets Multimedia, 800-331-6198. A more ambitious feature version made in Yugoslavia (120 minutes, 1969) features an international cast. It is available from Filmic Archives, 800-366-1920.

A Woman Called Moses. 200 minutes. Xenon, 1989. A made-for-TV docudrama with Cecily Tyson as Harret Tubman. It is based on the novel by Marcy Heldish. Available from Filmic Archives, 800-366-1920, and Social Studies School Service, 800-421-4246 or http://socialstudies.com.

Sitting Bull, or Tatanka-Iyotanka, was born about 1831 in what is today South Dakota. Sitting Bull was a Hunkpapa Lakota (Sioux), and as a young man he became a leader of the Strong Heart warrior society. He participated in his first battle at the age of 14. By 1870 he had become a respected warrior who had fought courageously against both Indian and American enemies. Sitting Bull was a Sioux holy man also noted for his spirituality. He was so admired by his people that, in 1876, the Lakota Sioux tribal leaders chose Sitting Bull as their war chief.

In 1868, the Sioux leader Red Cloud had signed the Treaty of Fort Laramie, which set up a Sioux reservation north of the Missouri River in the Dakotas. Other Sioux leaders did not accept the treaty. Sitting Bull, as well as chiefs Crazy Horse and Gall, wandered as he pleased on the unceded Indian lands. The Black Hills in the Dakota Territory were sacred to many tribes and were off-limits to white settlement, according to the terms of the Fort Laramie Treaty. Matters were brought to a head when the army decided to build a fort in the Black Hills to guard the Northern Pacific Railroad. Colonel George Armstrong Custer led an expedition to find a good location for the fort and confirmed that there was gold in the Black Hills. With thousands of prospectors and other settlers rushing into the Black Hills, the government put pressure on the Sioux to sell the Black Hills. The commissioner of Indian affairs decided that Sitting Bull and his peo-

ple had to be made to stay on the Sioux reservation.

During the spring of 1876, the United States army began a campaign to force the Cheyenne and Sioux off the plains and onto reservations. As soldiers began to move into his territory, Sitting Bull brought together the Sioux, Cheyenne, and Arapahoe to his camp and led them in the sun dance ritual and prayers to their Great Spirit. On June 25, 1876, at the Little Bighorn River in Montana, Crazy Horse, the Oglala Lakota war chief, and other warriors met an attack by Custer's forces and won a total victory, killing Custer and his five companies of men.

To the United States government, this was a great national embarrassment, since it occurred during the Centennial Year, a celebration of American greatness. Sitting Bull and his followers were pursued with a vengeance. Most Sioux were forced onto the reservation. Sitting Bull and a band of followers fled to Canada.

In 1881, finding it impossible to feed his people, Sitting Bull accepted amnesty and returned to the United States.

First sent to the Standing Rock Reservation in North Dakota, he was then transferred to prison at Fort Randall to calm fears that he might cause an uprising. After two years he was released to rejoin the tribe at Standing Rock. On the reservation, he remained a symbol of the opposition to white encroachment upon the traditional lands of the Sioux. Young Indians looked to him as a leader and built their tepees and cabins near his. During this time, Sitting Bull was be-friended by William "Buffalo Bill" Cody and toured with his Wild West Show in 1885.

In 1889–90, a new religion, the Ghost Dance, swept across the Indian tribes of the West. Originating with a medicine man named Wokova, the Ghost Dance religion taught that if the Indians danced in a new rit-ual, whites would disappear, Indian ancestors would return to life, and the buffalo would once more dominate the plains. Government authorities feared that the Ghost Dance would incite the Indians to go back to war. When Sit-ting Bull's followers began to make, for the ceremony, special shirts that were supposed to protect them from bullets, the chief was blamed for causing unrest.

On December 15, 1890, government offi-cials sent a party of Indian policemen to arrest Sitting Bull. The first group of Indian police had resigned rather than face the Sioux leader. These new police were also afraid of a confrontation. A disaster did occur, a scuffle broke out, and Sit-ting Bull and seven of his followers were killed. Even after his death, Sitting Bull's fame as a leader was such that the cabin where he was killed was displayed at the Chicago World's Fair in 1893. For many people who had read ac-counts of the Battle of Little Bighorn or had seen him in the Wild West Show, Sitting Bull re-mained the symbolic American Indian Chief.

Key Questions About This Subject

- Did the Sioux have legal rights to the Black Hills in the Dakotas?
- Why did the United States decide to ignore the terms of the Fort Laramie Treaty?
- What economic considerations caused white settlers to flood into Indian territory?
- What was Custer's role in this?
- Why did the government wish to move the Sioux and other tribes into reservations?

- Did Custer have any ulterior motives for wanting a dramatic victory over the western Indians?
- What was the ultimate fate of the Sioux people?
- What was the ultimate fate of Sitting Bull?
- What was the impact on the public in 1876 of Custer's defeat at Little Bighorn?
- On whose side would public opinion today likely fall—that of Custer or that of Sitting Bull?

Mock Trial

If you are going to hold a simulated trial, here are the charges against Sitting Bull (the Defendant): Sitting Bull, War Chief of the Lakota Sioux, is charged with leading a confederation of Sioux and Cheyenne warriors against Lieutenant Colonel George Arm-strong Custer and his soldiers that resulted in the death of Custer and approximately 260 of his men.

Critical Thinking Using Primary Sources in U.S. History

Document A

"From Far Dakota's Cañons", June 25, 1876

(From Walt Whitman's *Leaves of Grass*, 1881 edition.)

From far Dakota's cañons,
Lands of the wild ravine, the dusky Sioux, the lonesome stretch, the silence,
Haply to-day a mournful wail, haply a trumpet-note for heroes.

The battle-bulletin,
The Indian ambuscade, the craft, the fatal environment,
The cavalry companies fighting to the last in sternest heroism,
In the midst of their little circle, with their slaughter'd horses for breast-works,
The fall of Custer and all his officers and men.

Continues yet the old, old legend of our race,
The loftiest of life upheld by death,
The ancient banner perfectly maintain'd,
O lesson opportune, O how I welcome thee!

As sitting in dark days,
Lone, sulky, through the time's thick murk looking in vain for light, for hope,
From unsuspected parts a fierce and momentary proof,
(The sun there at the centre though conceal'd,
Electric life forever at the centre,)
Breaks forth a lightning flash.

Thou of the tawny flowing hair in battle,
I erewhile saw, with erect head, pressing ever in front, bearing a bright sword in thy hand,
Now ending well in death the splendid fever of thy deeds,
(I bring no dirge for it or thee, I bring a glad triumphal sonnet,)
Desperate and glorious, aye in defeat most desperate, most glorious,
After thy many battles in which never yielding up a gun or a color,
Leaving behind thee a memory sweet to soldiers,
Thou yieldest up thyself.

Mrs. Spotted Horn Bull: A View from the Village

(From James McLaughlin, *My Friend the Indian*. Boston: Houghton Mifflin, 1910, pp.167–172. As found in Colin G. Calloway, ed., *Our Hearts Fell to the Ground: Plains Indian Views of How the West Was Lost*. Boston: Bedford Books, 1996, pp. 146–148.)

> **Note:** This extract is a contemporary narrative of a witness to Custer's Last Stand.

Like that the soldiers were upon us. Through the tepee poles their bullets rattled. The sun was several hours high and the tepees were empty. Bullets coming from a strip of timber on the west bank of the Greasy Grass passed through the tepees of the Blackfeet and Hunkpapa. The broken character of the country across the river, together with the fringe of trees on the west side, where our camp was situated, had hidden the advance of a great number of soldiers, which we had not seen until they were close upon us and shooting into our end of the village, where, from seeing the direction taken by the soldiers we were watching, we felt comparatively secure.

The women and children cried, fearing they would be killed, but the men, the Hunkpapa and Blackfeet, the Oglala and Minniconjou, mounted their horses and raced to the Blackfeet tepees. We could still see the soldiers of Long Hair [Custer] marching along in the distance, and our men, taken by surprise, and from a point whence they had not expected to be attacked, went singing the song of battle into the fight behind the Blackfeet village. And we women wailed over the children, for we believed that the Great Father [President of the United States] had sent all his men for the destruction of the Sioux. Some of the women put loads on the travois* and would have left, but that their husbands and sons were in the fight. Others tore their hair and wept for the fate that they thought was to be the portion of the Sioux, through the anger of the Great Father, but their men were not afraid, and they had many guns and cartridges. Like the fire that, driven by a great wind, sweeps through the heavy grass-land where the buffalo range, the men of the Hunkpapa, the Blackfeet, the Oglala, and the Minniconjou rushed through the village and into the trees, where the soldiers of the white chief had stopped to fire. The soldiers [Reno's] had been sent by Long Hair to surprise the village of my people. . . .

From a hill behind the camp, at first, and then from the bank of the river, I watched the men of our people plan to overthrow the soldiers of the Great Father; and before a shot was fired, I knew that no man who rode with Long Hair would go back to tell the tale. . . .

From across the river I could hear the music of the bugle and could see the column of soldiers turn to the left to march down to the river to where the attack was to be made. All I could see was the warriors of my people. They rushed like the wind through the village, . . . There had been no council the night before—there was no need for one; nor had there been a scalp-dance. . . . When we did not know there was to be a fight, we could not be prepared for it. . . .

I cannot remember the time. When men fight and the air is filled with bullets, when the screaming of horses that are shot drowns the war-whoop of warriors, a woman whose husband and brothers are in the battle does not think of the time. But the sun was no longer overhead when the war-whoop of the Sioux sounded from the river-bottom and the rave surrounding the hill at the end of the ridge where Long Hair had taken his last stand. The river was in sight from the butte, and while the whoop

*Vehicle used by Plains Indians made of two trailing poles with a net or platform between for loads.

Critical Thinking Using
Primary Sources in U.S. History

still rung in our ears and the women were shrieking, two Cheyennes tried to cross the river and one of them was shot and killed by Long Hair's men. Then the men of the Sioux nation, led by Crow King, Hump, Crazy Horse, and many great chiefs, rose up on all sides of the hill, and the last we could see from our side of the river was a great number of gray horses. The smoke of the shooting and the dust of the horses shut out the hill, and the soldiers fired many shots, but the Sioux shot straight and the soldiers fell dead. The women crossed the river after the men of our village, and when we came to the hill there were no soldiers living and Long Hair lay dead among the rest. There were more than two hundred dead soldiers on the hill, and the boys of the village shot many who were already dead, for the blood of the people was hot and their hearts bad, and they took no prisoners that day.

Document C

Red Cloud's Speech to the Secretary of the Interior, 1870

(From *First Annual Report of the Board of Indian Commissioners for 1870.* Washington, D.C.: U.S. Government Printing Office, 1871, p. 41. As found in Colin G. Calloway, ed., *Our Hearts Fell to the Ground: Plains Indian Views of How the West Was Lost.* Boston: Bedford Books, 1996, pp. 154–155.)

The Great Spirit has seen me naked; and my Great Father, I have fought against him. I offered my prayers to the Great Spirit so I could come here safe. Look at me. I was raised on this land where the sun rises—now I come from where the sun sets. Whose voice was first sounded on this land? The voice of the red people, who had but bows and arrows. This Great Father says he is good and kind to us. I don't think so. I am good to his white people. From the word sent me I have come all the way to his home. My face is red; yours is white. The Great Spirit has made you to read and write, but not me. I have not learned. I come here to tell my Great Father what I do not like in my country. You are all close to my Great Father, and are a great many chiefs. The men the Great Father sends to us have no sense—no heart. What has been done in my country I did not want, did not ask for it; white people going through my country. Father, have you, or any of your friends here, got children? Do you want to raise them? Look at me; I come here with all these young men. All of them have children and want to raise them. The white children have surrounded me and have left me nothing but an island. When we first had this land we were strong, now we are melting like snow on the hillside, while you are grown like spring grass. Now I have come a long distance to my Great Father's house—see if I have left any blood in his land when I go. When the white man comes in my country he leaves a trail of blood behind him. Tell Great Father to move Fort Fetterman away and we will have no more trouble. I have two mountains in that country—the Black Hills and the Big Horn Mountain. I want the Great Father to make no roads through them. I have told these things three times; now I have come here to tell them the fourth time.

I do not want my reservation on the Missouri; this is the fourth time I have said so. Here are some people from there now. Our children are dying off like sheep; the country does not suit them. I was born at the forks of the Platte, and I was told that the land belonged to me from north, south, east, and west. The red man has come to the Great Father's house. The Ogallallas are the last who have come here; but I come to hear and listen to the words of the Great Father. They have promised me traders, but we have none. At the mouth of Horse Creek they had made a treaty in 1862 [probably the Treaty of Fort Laramie of 1868], and the man who made the treaty is the only one who has

Critical Thinking Using Primary Sources in U.S. History

told me truths. When you send goods to me, they are stolen all along the road, so when they reached me they were only a handful. They held a paper for me to sign, and that is all I got for my lands. I know the people you send out there are liars. Look at me. I am poor and naked. I do not want war with my Government. The railroad is passing through my country now; I have received no pay for the land—not even a brass ring. I want you to tell all this to my Great Father.

Document D

The Fort Laramie Treaty with the Sioux (Lakota), 1868 (Excerpts)

(As found in Albert L. Hurtado and Peter Iverson, eds., *Major Problems in American Indian History.* Lexington, MA: D.C. Heath, 1994.)

Article 1. From this day forward all war between the parties to this agreement shall forever cease. The Government of the United States desires peace, and its honor is hereby pledged to keep it. The Indians desire peace, and they now pledge their honor to maintain it.

If bad men among the whites, or among other people subject to the authority of the United States, shall commit any wrong upon the person or property of the Indians, the United States will, upon proof made to the agent and forwarded to the Commissioner of Indian Affairs at Washington City, proceed at once to cause the offender to be arrested and punished according to the laws of the United States, and also re-imburse the injured person for the loss sustained.

If bad men among the Indians shall commit a wrong or depredation upon the person or property of any one, white, black, or Indian, subject to the authority of the United States, and at peace therewith, the Indians herein named solemnly agree that they will, upon proof made to their agent and notice by him, deliver up the wrong-doer to the United States, to be tried and punished according to its laws; and in case they wilfully refuse to do so, the person injured shall be reimbursed for his loss. . . .

Article 7. In order to insure the civilization of the Indians entering into this treaty, the necessity of education is admitted . . . and they therefore pledge themselves to compel their children, male and female, between the ages of six and sixteen years, to attend school . . . and the United States agree that for every thirty children between said ages who can be induced or compelled to attend school, a house shall be provided and a teacher competent to teach the elementary branches of an English education shall be furnished, who will reside among said Indians, and faithfully discharge his or her duties as a teacher. . . .

Article 16. The United States hereby agrees and stipulates that the country north of the North Platte River and east of the summits of the Big Horn Mountains shall be held and considered to be unceded Indian territory, and also stipulates and agrees that no white person or persons shall be permitted to settle upon or occupy any portion of the same; or without the consent of the Indians first had and obtained, to pass through the same; and it is further agreed by the United States that within ninety days after the conclusion of peace with all the bands of the Sioux Nation, the military posts now established in the territory in this article named shall be abandoned, and that the road leading to them and by them to the settlements in the Territory of Montana shall be closed.

Our Life's Last Chapter (Excerpts)

(As found in Elizabeth B. Custer, *"Boots and Saddles" or, Life in Dakota with General Custer.* Norman: University of Oklahoma Press, 1961, p. 216–224. Originally published in 1885.)

Our women's hearts fell when the fiat went forth that there was to be a summer campaign, with probably actual fighting with the Indians. . . .

Sitting Bull refused to make a treaty with the government and would not come in to live on a reservation. Besides his constant attacks on the white settlers, driving back even the most adventurous, he was incessantly invading and stealing from the land assigned to the peaceable Crows. They appealed for help to the government that had promised to shield them. . . .

A picture of one day of our life in those disconsolate times is fixed indelibly in my memory.

On Sunday afternoon, June 25, our little group of saddened women, borne down with one common weight of anxiety, sought solace in gathering together in our house. We tried to find some slight surcease from trouble in the old hymns; some of them dated back to our childhood's days, when our mothers rocked us to sleep to their soothing strains. I remember the grief with which one fair young wife threw herself on the carpet and pillowed her head in the lap of a tender friend. Another sat dejected at the piano and struck soft chords that melted into the notes of the voices. All were absorbed in the same thoughts, and their eyes were filled with faraway visions and longings. Indescribable yearning for the absent, and untold terror for their safety, engrossed each heart. The words of the hymn,

E'en though a cross it be
Nearer, my God, to Thee,

came forth with almost a sob from every throat.

At that very hour the fears that our tortured minds had portrayed in imagination were realities, and the souls of those we thought upon were ascending to meet their Maker. On July 5—for it took that time for the news to come—the sun rose on a beautiful world, but with its earliest beams came the first knell of disaster. A steamer came down the river, bearing the wounded from the battle of the Little Big Horn, of Sunday, June 25. This battle wrecked the lives of twenty-six women at Fort Lincoln, and orphaned children of officers and soldiers joined the cry to that of their bereaved mothers.

From that time the life went out of the hearts of the "women who weep," and God asked them to walk on alone and in the shadow.

Resources

Bibliography

Ambrose, Stephen E. *Crazy Horse and Custer: The Parallel Lives of Two American Warriors*. Baltimore: Anchor Press, 1996.

Bachrach, Deborah. *Custer's Last Stand: Opposing Viewpoints*. San Diego: Greenhaven Press, 1990.

Calloway, Colin G., ed. *Our Hearts Fell to the Ground: Plains Indian Views of How the West Was Lost*. Boston: Bedford Books, 1996.

Carroll, John M., ed. *The Benteen-Goldin Letters on Custer and His Last Battle*. Lincoln: University of Nebraska, 1991.

Connell, Evan S. *Son of the Morning Star: Custer and the Little Bighorn*. North Point Press, 1984.

Frazier, Ian. *Great Plains*. New York: Farrar, Strauss, Giroux, 1989.

Gray, John Stephens, et al. *Centennial Campaign: The Sioux War of 1876*. Norman: University of Oklahoma Press, 1988.

Greene, Jerome A. *Battles and Skirmishes of the Great Sioux War, 1876–1877: The Military View*. Norman: University of Oklahoma Press, 1996.

Greene, Jerome A. *Lakota and Cheyenne: Indian Views of the Great Sioux War, 1876–1877*. Norman: University of Oklahoma, 1994.

Oehler, C.M. *The Great Sioux Uprising*. New York: Da Capo Press, 1997.

Robinson, Charles M. *A Good Year to Die: The Story of the Great Sioux War*. Norman: University of Oklahoma Press, 1996.

Utley, Robert M. *Cavalier in Buckskin: George Armstrong Custer and the Western Military Frontier*. Norman: University of Oklahoma Press, 1991.

Utley, Robert M. *Last Days of the Sioux Nation*. New Haven: Yale University Press, 1963.

Viola, Herman J., and Charles Shaw. *Sitting Bull*. Austin: Steck-Vaughn, 1996.

Wert, Jeffrey D. *Custer: The Controversial Life of George Armstrong Custer*. New York: Simon and Schuster, 1996.

Media Resources

Documentaries

500 Nations. 49 minutes each part. Columbia House, 1994. Eight-part documentary series, with volume 7 dealing specifically with Sitting Bull. Available from Zenger Media, 800-421-4246.

How the West Was Lost. 300 minutes. Discovery Channel program, 1993. Available from Zenger Media, 800-421-4246.

Last Stand at Little Big Horn: Tribal Legacies Series. 60 minutes. PBS program, 1992. Available from Zenger Media, 800-421-4246.

The Way West. 6 hours. Four-part series by Ric Burns. Concerns the clash between settlers and Native Americans. Available from PBS Video, 800-344-3337.

Feature Films

Little Big Man. 150 minutes. Swank Motion Pictures/Key Video, 1970. Stars Dustin Hoffman. The sole survivor of Custer's Last Stand relates his life story in both the Indian's and white man's worlds. Available at many video stores.

Son of the Morning Star. 183 minutes. 1991. Based on the book of the same title, this film features a dual veiwpoint of the Battle of Little Big Horn. Available from Zenger Media, 800-421-4246.

UNIT 7 | William McKinley and the Spanish-American War

HISTORICAL BACKGROUND

William McKinley was the seventh child of William and Nancy McKinley, born in Ohio in 1843. He spent his childhood in Poland, Ohio. After a brief stay in Allegheny College, he enlisted in the Union army at the outbreak of the Civil War, seeing action with the Twenty-third Ohio Volunteer Regiment in the Shenandoah Valley and at Antietam. McKinley left the army with the brevet (temporary) rank of major. Returning home, he studied for the bar and opened his own legal practice in 1867, becoming Stark county prosecutor in 1869. McKinley married in 1871, though the couple's two children died and the strain left his wife, Ida, an invalid.

McKinley ran for Congress in 1876 as a Republican and served in the House for fourteen years. His political career advanced rapidly in the House, though he lost the race for the speakership in 1889 to Thomas Reed. After a brief stint as Chairman of the House Ways and Means Committee, McKinley lost his House seat in the Democratic landslide of 1890. McKinley then won the governorship of Ohio in 1891, serving two terms and firmly establishing himself on the national political scene.

McKinley positioned himself as the front-runner for the Republican nomination for president in the 1896 election, winning the party nomination on the first ballot. McKinley soundly defeated the Democratic nominee, William Jennings Bryan, and took office in 1897. Although the campaign had focused on domestic issues, foreign policy would dominate his presidency. Spain had been engaged in suppressing a revolt in Cuba, and the American press was making it into a political issue by calling for American intervention. McKinley at first brought diplomatic pressure to bear on the Spanish, but they refused to grant Cuban independence. Then, the American battleship *Maine* sank in Havana harbor. It was probably the result of an accident on board the ship, though at the time the press encouraged the popular beleif that the sinking resulted from Spanish sabotage. This sinking, on top of Spanish refusal to negotiate, led to a congressional declaration of war.

Although the struggle grew out of the Cuban revolt, American forces also took Puerto Rico and the Philippines during the brief war. Cuba gained nominal independence in 1902, but the issue of the Philippines proved much more difficult. McKinley directed Admiral Dewey to seize the islands at the outbreak of the war because of their strategic importance in the Pacific. McKinley (who hinted that he had received divine guidance on the matter) convinced Congress to accept the American annexation of the islands despite strong opposition from anti-imperialists. Filipinos fought back through an independence movement led by Emilio Aguinaldo. American troops crushed the movement, using many of the same tactics that the Spanish had used during the Cuban revolt to much public outcry. McKinley, this time with "Rough Rider" hero Theodore Roosevelt as his running mate, again defeated Bryan in the 1900 election and began to call for a more global role for America. In 1901 an anarchist assassinated McKinley, and Roosevelt became president.

Key Questions About This Subject

- How did President McKinley justify his decision to annex the Philippines at the end of the Spanish-American War?
- What was the imperialist context within which the American decision was made?
- What arguments were made in the Senate both for and against this annexation?
- Why did the leaders of the Filipino revolt against the Spanish feel betrayed by the American action?
- Were the Filipinos justified in resisting the American occupation?

Mock Trial

If you are going to hold a simulated trial, here are the charges against President William McKinley (the Defendant): U.S. President William McKinley is accused of annexing by force the Philippine Islands, against the wishes of the Filipino population, and causing, by that annexation, the deaths of thousands of Filipinos in the resulting U.S. military pacification.

DOCUMENTS

Document A

Remarks by President William McKinley to a Methodist Delegation, November 21, 1899

(From General James Rusling, "Interview with President William McKinley." *The Christian Advocate,* New York, January 22,1903, p. 17.)

Hold a moment longer! Not quite yet, gentlemen! Before you go I would like to say just a word about the Philippine business. I have been criticized a good deal about the Philippines, but don't deserve it. The truth is I didn't want the Philippines, and when they came to us, as a gift from the gods, I did not know what to do with them. When the Spanish War broke out Dewey was at Hongkong, and I ordered him to go to Manila and to capture or destroy the Spanish fleet, and he had to; because, if defeated, he had no place to refit on that side of the globe, and if the Dons were victorious they would likely cross the Pacific and ravage our Oregon and California coasts. And so he had to destroy the Spanish fleet, and did it! But that was as far as I thought then.

When I next realized that the Philippines had dropped into our laps I confess I did not know what to do with them. I sought counsel from all sides—Democrats as well as Republicans—but got little help. I thought first we would take only Manila; then Luzon; then other islands perhaps also. I walked the floor of the White House night after night until midnight; and I am not ashamed to tell you, gentlemen, that I went down on my knees and prayed Almighty God for light and guidance more than one night. And one night late it came to me this way—I don't know how it was, but it came: (1) That we could not give them back to Spain—that would be cowardly and dishonorable; (2) that we could not turn them over to France and Germany—our commercial rivals in the Orient—that would be bad business and discreditable; (3) that we could not leave them to themselves—they were unfit for self-government—and they would soon have anarchy and misrule over there worse than Spain's was; and (4) that there was nothing left for us to do but to take them all, and to educate the Filipinos, and uplift and civilize and Christianize them, and by God's grace do the very best we could by them, as our fellow-men for whom Christ also died. And then I went to bed, and went to sleep, and slept soundly, and the next morning I sent for the chief engineer of the War Department (our map-maker), and I told him to put the Philippines on the map of the United States (pointing to a large map on the wall of his office), and there they are, and there they will stay while I am President!"

Document B

The War Message: President Emilio Aguinaldo, February 4, 1899

(From Senate Document 208, 56th Congress, 1st Session [February 4,1899], p. 104.)

Nine o'clock p.m., this date, I received from Caloocan station a message communicated to me that American forces, without prior notification or any just motive, attacked our camp at San Juan del Monte and our forces garrisoning the blockhouses around the outskirts of Manila, causing losses among our soldiers, who, in view of this unexpected aggression and of the decided attack of the ag-gressors, were obliged to defend themselves until the firing became general all along the line.

No one can deplore more than I this rupture of hostilities. I have a clear conscience that I have endeavored to avoid it at all costs, using all my efforts to preserve friendship with the army of occu-pation, even at the cost of not a few humiliations and many sacrificed rights.

But it is my unavoidable duty to maintain the integrity of the national honor and that of the army so unjustly attacked by those who, posing as our friends and liberators, attempted to domi-nate us in place of the Spaniards, as is shown by the grievances enumerated in my manifest of Janu-ary 8 last; such as the continued outrages and violent exactions committed against the people of Manila, the useless conferences, and all my frustrated efforts in favor of peace and concord.

Summoned by this unexpected provocation, urged by the duties imposed upon me by honor and patriotism and for the defense of the nation intrusted to me, calling on God as a wit-ness of my good faith and the uprightness of my intentions—
I order and command:

1. Peace and friendly relations between the Philippine forces and the American forces of oc-cupation are broken, and the latter will be treated as enemies, with the limits prescribed by the laws of war.
2. American soldiers who may be captured by the Philippine forces will be treated as prisoners of war.
3. This proclamation shall be communicated to the accredited consuls of Manila, and to congress, in order that it may accord the suspension of the constitutional guaranties and the resulting declaration of war.

Given at Malolos, February 4,1899

Emilio Aguinaldo,
General in Chief

Critical Thinking Using Primary Sources in U.S. History

Speech of Senator Benjamin Tillman, February 7, 1899

(From *Congressional Record*, 55th Congress, 3rd Session [February 7, 1899], pp. 1530–1532.)

As I understand the legal status the ratification of the treaty will bring about this result: That in the eye of the law the Philippine Islands are ours and the inhabitants thereof are to-day rebels; they are now ours by right of cession from Spain, ratified yesterday by this body, and to be ratified soon by the Spanish Government; they are American subjects; and since they have fired upon the flag they are "rebels." That is the law of the situation as we see it and possibly as the world sees it.

Now, considering the fact, which can not be denied—for our consul, Mr. Williams, reported the fact as far back as February, 1898, before Dewey sailed into Manila Bay—that there was a rebellion against Spain: that the Filipino army was lying outside of the city of Manila and hostilities were active; considering the fact that they organized a government as far back as last June; considering the fact that they have been actively engaged in collecting munitions of war and have recruited their army until, as this officer told me, they have not less than 40,000 men outside of Manila to-day, we are brought face to face with the consideration as to whether it was not wise and proper and the best thing from their point of view for the Filipinos to make the attack which they did, or which it is said they did, on Saturday night last.

If they went to war with the United States before the United States had a title to those islands in law, what is their legal status in international law? They can not be called rebels to us except from the extreme standpoint of legal technicality. We had no right in Manila so far as they were concerned; we only had rights there so far as Spain was concerned; and if, after they had their representative here pleading and begging for some word of comfort, some promise as to our policy, or some dim outline even as to the purpose of recognizing their right to local self-government, they grew desperate at last and fired upon our troops, the firing upon those troops before we had any legal title must give them the right of belligerents in war, although they have been subjects of Spain, because by the cession to us we simply fall heir to Spain's residuary title in those islands, subject to the rights of the natives who were struggling for freedom before we went to war with Spain on an entirely different issue.

We may say they are rebels, and in strict legal interpretation they may be rebels, but, Mr. President, let this war terminate how it will, history will declare that they are to-day patriots striving for what we fought for in our struggle with Great Britain in the last century; and we can not escape from the condition at least of doubt as to the course we ought to follow when we consider this fact. They were fighting for their freedom against Spanish tyranny two years ago, and they continued to fight up to the time when Aguinaldo left the islands and went to Singapore; they continued the fight, as our own consul said, after he left; they never did cease, some of them; there never was peace; and now the question which addresses itself to every American who loves his flag and loves his great country and loves the great principle upon which that flag rests and that country is founded is this: Are we to take the place of Spain as their taskmasters and oppressors? Do "governments derive their powers from the consent of the governed"? . . .

We can send troops enough to Manila to kill, as the Senator from Montana (Mr. Carter) said the other day, "to shoot them to death," if need be, to make them respect our flag and our authority. We can do it. Nobody doubts that. The question is ought we to do it? Is it honorable to do it? Is it right to do it?

Document D

Excerpts from the Proclamation of the U.S. Commission Toward Conciliation and the Establishment of Peace

(Issued at Manila, April 4, 1899. English version published by the U.S. Government Printing Office, Vol. 1, January 31, 1900.)

To the people of the Philippine Islands:

. . . The Commission desire to assure the people of the Philippine Islands of the cordial good will and fraternal feeling which is entertained for them by His Excellency the President of the United States and by the American people. The aim and object of the American Government, apart from the fulfillment of the solemn obligations it has assumed toward the family of nations by the acceptance of sovereignty over the Philippine Islands, is the well being, the prosperity, and the happiness of the Philippine people and their elevation and advancement to a position among the most civilized peoples of the world.

His Excellency the President of the United States believes that this felicity and perfection of the Philippine people is to be brought about by the assurance of peace and order; by the guaranty of civil and religious liberty; by the establishment of justice; . . . in a word, by the uninterrupted devotion of the people to the pursuit of those useful objects and the realization of those noble ideals which constitute the higher civilization of mankind.

Unfortunately, the pure aims and purposes of the American Government and people have been misinterpreted to some of the inhabitants of certain of the islands. As a consequence, the friendly American forces have, without provocation or cause, been openly attacked.

And why these hostilities? What do the best Filipinos desire? Can it be more than the United States is ready to give? They are patriots and want liberty, it is said. The Commission emphatically asserts that the United States is not only willing, but anxious, to establish in the Philippine Islands an enlightened system of government under which the Philippine people may enjoy the largest measure of home rule and the amplest liberty consonant with the supreme ends of government and compatible with those obligations which the United States has assumed toward the civilized nations of the world. . . .

It is the expectation of the commission to visit the Philippine peoples in their respective provinces, both for the purpose of cultivating a more intimate mutual acquaintance and also with a view to ascertaining from enlightened native opinion what form or forms of government seem best adapted to the Philippine peoples, most apt to conduce to their highest welfare, and most conformable to their customs, traditions, sentiments, and cherished ideals. . . .

In the meantime the attention of the Philippine people is invited to certain regulative principles by which the United States will be guided in its relations with them. The following are deemed of cardinal importance:

1. The supremacy of the United States must and will be enforced throughout every part of the Archipelago, and those who resist it can accomplish no end other than their own ruin.

2. The most ample liberty of self-government will be granted to the Philippine people which is reconcilable with the maintenance of a wise, just, stable, effective, and economical administration of public affairs, and compatible with the sovereign and international rights and obligations of the United States.

3. The civil rights of the Philippine people will be guaranteed and protected to the fullest extent; religious freedom assured, and all persons shall have an equal standing before the law.

4. Honor, justice, and friendship forbid the use of the Philippine people or islands as an object or means of exploitation. The purpose of the American Government is the welfare and advancement of the Philippine people.

5. There shall be guaranteed to the Philippine people an honest and effective civil service, in which, to the fullest extent practicable, natives shall be employed.

6. The collection and application of taxes and revenues will be put upon a sound, honest, and economical basis. . . .

7. A pure, speedy, and effective administration of justice will be established, whereby the evils of delay, corruption, and exploitation will be effectually eradicated.

8. The construction of roads, railroads, and other means of communication and transportation, as well as other public works of manifest advantage to the Philippine people, will be promoted.

9. Domestic and foreign trade and commerce, agriculture, and other industrial pursuits, and the general development of the country in the interest of its inhabitants will be constant objects of solicitude and fostering care.

10. Effective provision will be made for the establishment of elementary schools in which the children of the people shall be educated. Appropriate facilities will also be provided for higher education.

11. Reforms in all departments of the government, in all branches of the public service, and in all corporations closely touching the common life of the people must be undertaken without delay. . . .

Jacob Gould Schurman,
President of the Commission

George Dewey,
Admiral, U.S. N[avy]

Ewell S. Otis,
Major-General, U.S. Volunteers

Charles Denby

Dean C. Worcester

John R. MacArthur
Secretary of Commission

"The White Man's Burden," Rudyard Kipling, 1899

(Referring to the United States and the Philippine Islands)

Take up the White Man's burden—
        Send forth the best ye breed—
Go bind your sons to exile
        To serve your captives' need;
To wait in heavy harness
        On fluttered folk and wild—
Your new-caught, sullen peoples,
        Half devil and half child.

Take up the White Man's burden—
        In patience to abide,
To veil the threat of terror
        And check the show of pride;
By open speech and simple,
        An hundred times made plain,
To seek another's profit,
        And work another's gain.

Take up the White Man's burden—
        The savage wars of peace—
Fill full the mouth of Famine
        And bid the sickness cease;
And when your goal is nearest
        The end for others sought,
Watch Sloth and heathen Folly
        Bring all your hope to nought.

Take up the White Man's burden—
        No tawdry rule of kings,
But toil of serf and sweeper—
        The tale of common things.
The ports ye shall not enter,
        The roads ye shall not tread,
Go make them with your living,
        And mark them with your dead!

Take up the White Man's burden—
    And reap his old reward:
The blame of those ye better,
    The hate of those ye guard—
The cry of hosts ye humour
    (Ah, slowly!) toward the light:—
'Why brought ye us from bondage,
    'Our loved Egyptian night?'

Take up the White Man's burden—
    Ye dare not stoop to less—
Nor call too loud on Freedom
    To cloak your weariness;
By all ye cry or whisper,
    By all ye leave or do,
The silent, sullen peoples
    Shall weigh your Gods and you.

Take up the White Man's burden—
    Have done with childish days—
The lightly proffered laurel,
    The easy, ungrudged praise.
Comes now, to search your manhood
    Through all the thankless years,
Cold-edged with dear-brought wisdom.
    The judgment of your peers!

Speech of Massachusetts Senator Henry Cabot Lodge, March 7, 1900

(From *The Congressional Record*, 60th Congress, 1st Session, Volume 33, Part 3, pp. 2618–2630.)

The policy we offer is simple and straightforward. We believe in the frank acceptance of existing facts, and in dealing with them as they are and not on a theory of what they might or ought to be. We accept the fact that the Philippine Islands are ours to-day and that we are responsible for them before the world. The next fact is that there is a war in those islands. Our immediate duty, therefore, is to suppress this disorder, put an end to fighting, and restore peace and order. That is what we are doing. . . .

I hope and believe that we shall retain the islands, and that, peace and order once restored, we shall and should reestablish civil government, beginning with the towns and villages, where the inhabitants are able to manage their own affairs. We should give them honest administration, and prompt and efficient courts. We should see to it that there is entire protection to persons and property, in order to encourage the development of the islands by the assurance of safety to investors of capital. All men should be protected in the free exercise of their religion, and the doors thrown open to missionaries of all Christian sects. The land, which belongs to the people, and of which they have been robbed in the past, should be returned to them and their titles made secure. We should inaugurate and carry forward, in the most earnest and liberal way, a comprehensive system of popular education. Finally, while we bring prosperity to the islands by developing their resources, we should, as rapidly as conditions permit, bestow upon them self-government and home rule. . . .

The foundation of it all is the retention of the Islands by the United States, and it is to that question that I desire to address myself. The opposition . . . assert that on moral grounds we have no right to take or retain the Philippines, and that as a matter of expediency our whole Eastern policy is a costly mistake. I deny both propositions. . . . I believe that to abandon the islands, or to leave them now, would be a wrong to humanity, a dereliction of duty. . . . As to expediency, the arguments in favor of the retention of the Philippines seem to me so overwhelming that I should regard their loss as a calamity to our trade and commerce and to all our business interests so great that no man can measure it. . . .

Our opponents put forward as their chief objection that we have robbed these people of their liberty and have taken them and hold them in defiance of the doctrine of the Declaration of Independence in regard to the consent of the governed. As to liberty, they have never had it, and have none now, except when we give it to them protected by the flag and the armies of the United States. Their insurrection against Spain, confined to one island, had been utterly abortive and could never have revived or been successful while Spain controlled the sea. We have given them all the liberty they ever had. We could not have robbed them of it, for they had none to lose. . . .

Resources

Bibliography

Bradford, James C., ed. *Crucible of Empire: The Spanish American War and Its Aftermath.* Annapolis, MD: Naval Institute Press, 1993.

Bain, David Howard. *Sitting in Darkness: Americans in the Philippines.* Boston: Houghton Mifflin, 1984.

Beisner, Robert. *Twelve Against Empire: The Anti-Imperialists, 1898–1902.* New York: McGraw-Hill, 1968.

Graham, Cosmos. *An Army for Empire: The U.S. Army in the Spanish American War.* Columbia: University of Missouri Press, 1971.

Karnow, Stanley. *In Our Image: America's Empire in the Philippines.* New York: Random House, 1989.

Gould, Lewis. *Presidency of William McKinley.* Lawrence, KS: Regents Press, 1980.

Musicant, Ivan. *Empire by Default: The Spanish-American War and the Dawn of the American Century.* New York: H. Holt, 1998.

Sievers, Harry Joseph. *William McKinley, 1843–1901: Chronology, Documents, Bibliographical Aids.* Dobbs Ferry, NY: Oceana Publications, 1970.

Tuchman, Barbara. *The Proud Tower: A Portrait of the World Before the War: 1890–1914.* New York: Macmillan, 1962.

Wolff, Leon. *Little Brown Brother.* New York: Doubleday, 1960.

Media Resources

Documentaries

Colonial Days. 60 minutes. 1989. The first episode in the PBS Series *The U.S. and the Philippines: In Our Image,* it covers the American occupation through World War II. Available from PBS Video, 800-344-3337.

Crucible of Empire: The Spanish-American War. 120 minutes. 1999. A two-part documentary in the PBS series *The American Experience.* Available from PBS Video, 800-344-3337.

History of the 20th Century: 1900–1909. 60 minutes. ABC Video. Compiled from a wide variety of documentary and dramatic sources, it contains material concerning the Philippine Insurrection as it covers the first decade of the century. The decade-by-decade series (through 1979) was originally released as *Our American Century.* Available from Zenger Media, 800-421-4246.

The Innocent Years. 54 minutes. 1957. Originally a Project XX documentary, NBC has repackaged it with an introduction by Tom Brokaw. It covers U.S. history from the Spanish-American War to World War I. Available from either Zenger Media, 800-421-4246, or Filmic Archives, 800-366-1920.

The Lure of Empire: America Debates Imperialism. 27 minutes. Using dialog excerpted from contemporary documents (some of which includes racial stereotyping), it explores American attitudes toward the Philippine annexation. Available from Social Studies School Service, 800-421-4246.

McKinley and American Imperialism. 25 minutes. 1992. The focus is specifically on McKinley's role. Available from the Educational Video Network, 1390 19th Street, Huntsville, TX 77340, 409-295-5767.

Savage Acts: Wars, Fairs, and Empire. 30 minutes. 1997. Explores the ideological link between the U.S. conquest of the Philippines and the World's Fair held at the turn of the century. Available from the American Social History Project, Center for Media and Learning, Graduate Center, City University of New York, 365 Fifth Avenue, New York, NY 10016, 212-817-1966.

The Spanish American War. 50 minutes. 1997. A History Channel overview of the war. Available from Teacher's Video Company, 800-262-8837.

The Spanish American War—Birth of a Super Power: As It Happened. 100 minutes. 1996. Arts and Entertainment (A&E) program combines documentary material with re-enactments. Available from Zenger Media, 800-421-4246.

The Spanish American War: The Dynamics of Change. 30 minutes. VHS filmstrip transfer that covers a number of the issues arising from the war, including the Philippine takeover. Available from Social Studies School Service, 800-421-4246.

The Splendid Little War. 55 minutes. 1992. Using early newsreels, still photos, dramatic re-enactments, and music, it provides an overview of the origins, prosecution, key figures, and outcomes of the Spanish-American War. It is available from Zenger Media, 800-421-4246.

Theodore Roosevelt: Roughrider to Rushmore. 50 minutes. Part of the Arts and Entertainment (A&E) series *Biography.* Available from Public Television, the Videofinder's Collection, 800-799-1199.

This Bloody, Blundering Business. 30 minutes. 1978. Deals specifically with the American suppression of the Philippine Insurrection. Available from Cinema Guild, 800-723-5522.

TR: The Story of Theodore Roosevelt. 240 minutes. 1996. A full-scale documentary on the life of the "rough rider" from his childhood to his death. Available from PBS Video, 800-344-3337.

Feature Films

Cavalry Command. 82 minutes. 1963. One of only two dramatic films that deal with the Philippine Insurrection. The other is *The True Glory* (95 minutes, 1939, not available on video). Both films are highly favorable to the U.S., setting noble U.S. army forces against evil guerrilla fighters to win the hearts and minds of the peasants. Available from Rhino Home Video, 800-843-3670.

Message to Garcia (77 minutes, 1936), *Yellow Jack* (83 minutes, 1938), and *Santiago* (93 minutes, 1956). Feature films that fictionalize aspects of the war in the Caribbean. None available on video.

Rough Riders. 240 minutes. 1997. Television film that focuses on Teddy Roosevelt's experiences forming his volunteer unit and fighting in Cuba. Available from Teacher's Video Company, 800-262-8837.

UNIT 8 | Henry Ford and the American Worker

Henry Ford was born in 1863 near Detroit, Michigan, the first of six children. Raised in a farm family, Ford developed an interest in machines. By 1880 Ford was working as a mechanic and began tinkering with the idea of a "horseless carriage." After his marriage to Clara Bryant, he began working for the Detroit Edison Illumination Company. It was there that he met Thomas Edison. In 1896, Ford developed a primitive car called a quadricycle, and Edison encouraged him to make further developments. Ford developed a gas-powered car in 1899 and decided to leave the Edison company.

In 1903 Ford founded the Ford Motor Company. In 1908 he produced the Model T car, which would dominate the industry. Ford developed the assembly line process (and the $5-a-day wage for his workers) to create a compliant and loyal semi-skilled workforce to mass-produce automobiles efficiently. The Model T would account for half of all the automobiles sold in the United States from 1918 through 1925. Ford's goal was to produce an automobile that the masses could afford. He accomplished his goal with the Model T. The cheap, mass-produced car that he pioneered was widely copied both at home and abroad, and the new "automobility" changed everything, from personal freedom, family relationships, and courtship patterns, to the shape of cities, the nature of work, the allure of suburbia, the focus of the economy, and the content of the air we breathe.

Automobiles were not Ford's only interest. He attempted unilaterally to mediate World War I in 1916, and tried to run for president of the United States in 1924. Although renowned as a philanthropist and reformer, Ford also tried to govern the private lives of his workers and was strongly anti-union. He was even accused of spreading crude anti-semitism through a newspaper that he owned. He also spent much time and money creating a replica of rural America at Greenfield Village, Dearborn, Michigan, an America that he had done so much to destroy. Ford died in 1947.

Key Questions About This Subject

- How did Henry Ford transform industrial work in the production of his Model T automobile?
- What benefits did Ford's workers derive from this organization?
- What did workers have to give up in order to work for Ford?

- What were the larger economic, political, social, and cultural consequences of Ford's making automobiles available to a majority of Americans?
- Which of these effects have been positive, how, and for whom? Which were negative, how, and for whom? What alternatives might have been possible?

Mock Trial

If you are going to hold a simulated trial, here are the charges against Henry Ford (the Defendant): Henry Ford (1863–1947), American industrialist, is accused of destroying the bond between the craftsman and his work, between the individual and his or her community, and between humanity and its environment. This stems from his development of the mass-produced automobile and the rootless mobility and energy dependence that it created.

DOCUMENTS

Document A

Narrative of Henry Ford

(From Henry Ford, *My Life and Work*. Garden City, NY: Doubleday, 1922, pp. 92–93, 104–106, 254–257.)

Now a business, in my way of thinking, is not a machine. It is a collection of people who are brought together to do work and not to write letters to one another. It is not necessary for any one department to know what any other department is doing. If a man is doing his work he will not have time to take up any other work. It is the business of those who plan the entire work to see that all of the departments are working properly toward the same end. It is not necessary to have meetings to establish good feeling between individuals or departments. It is not necessary for people to love each other in order to work together. Too much good fellowship may indeed be a very bad thing, for it may lead to one man trying to cover up the faults of another. That is bad for both men. . . .

We make the individual responsibility complete. The workman is absolutely responsible for his work. The straw boss is responsible for the workmen under him. The foreman is responsible for his group. The department head is responsible for the department. The general superintendent is responsible for the whole factory. Every man has to know what is going on in his sphere. . . .

Because there are no titles and no limits of authority, there is no question of red tape or going over a man's head. Any workman can go to anybody, and so established has become this custom, that a foreman does not get sore if a workman goes over him and goes directly to the head of the factory. The workman rarely ever does so, because a foreman knows as well as he knows his own name that if he has been unjust it will be very quickly found out, and he shall no longer be a foreman. One of the things that we will not tolerate is injustice of any kind. The moment a man starts to swell with authority he is discovered, and he goes out, or goes back to a machine. A large amount of labour unrest comes from the unjust exercise of authority by those in subordinate positions and I am afraid that in far too many manufacturing institutions it is really not possible for a workman to get a square deal. . . .

If a man cannot earn his keep without the aid of machinery, is it benefitting him to withhold that machinery because attendance upon it may be monotonous? And let him starve? Or is it better to put him in the way of a good living? Is a man the happier for starving? If he is the happier for using a machine to less than its capacity, is he happier for producing less than he might and consequently getting less than his share of the world's goods in exchange?

I have not been able to discover that repetitive labour injures a man in any way. . . . It would seem reasonable to imagine that going through the same set of motions daily for eight hours would produce an abnormal body, but we have never had a case of it. We shift men whenever they ask to be shifted and we should like regularly to change them—that would be entirely feasible if only the men would have it that way. They do not like changes which they do not themselves suggest. . . .

The most thorough research has not brought out a single case of a man's mind being twisted or deadened by the work. The kind of mind that does not like repetitive work does not have to stay in it. . . .

The only strong group of union men in the country is the group that draws salaries from the unions. Some of them are very rich. Some of them are interested in influencing the affairs of our large institutions of finance. Others are so extreme in their so-called socialism that they border on Bolshevism and anarchism—their union salaries liberating them from the necessity of work so that they can devote their energies to subversive propaganda. All of them enjoy a certain prestige and power which, in the natural course of competition, they could not otherwise have won.

If the official personnel of the labour unions were as strong, as honest, as decent, and as plainly wise as the bulk of the men who make up the membership, the whole movement would have taken on a different complexion these last few years. But this official personnel, in the main—there are notable exceptions—has not devoted itself to an alliance with the naturally strong qualities of the workingman; it has rather devoted itself to playing upon his weakness. . . .

The only true labour leader is the one who leads labour to work and to wages, and not the leader who leads labour to strikes, sabotage, and starvation. The union of labour which is coming to the fore in this country is the union of all whose interests are interdependent—whose interests are altogether dependent on the usefulness and efficiency of the service they render.

There is a change coming. When the union of "union leaders" disappears, with it will go the union of blind bosses—bosses who never did a decent thing for their employees until they are compelled. . . .

I am not opposed to labour organization. I am not opposed to any sort of organization that makes for progress. It is organizing to limit production—whether by employers or by workers—that matters.

The workingman himself must be on guard against some very dangerous notions—dangerous to himself and to the welfare of the country. It is sometimes said that the less a worker does, the more jobs he creates for other men. This fallacy assumes that idleness is creative. Idleness never created a job. It creates only burdens. The industrious man never runs his fellow worker out of a job; indeed, it is the industrious man who is the partner of the industrious manager— who creates more and more business and therefore more and more jobs.

Magazine Article

(From Don Sherman, "Willow Run: When Henry Ford was finally persuaded to build B-24s, he did it his way—mass production at full throttle." *Air & Space*. Washington, D.C., Smithsonian Institution, August/September, 1992, pp. 74, 76–84.)

At the outbreak of World War II, Henry Ford was an elderly, unpredictable man riddled with contradictions. He was far ahead of his time in paying workers five dollars a day, but he resisted to the bitter end their efforts to unionize. He was often spiteful toward his only son, Edsel, but never failed to dote on his four grandchildren. Although he saw involvement in a European war as part of a conspiracy against him and his company, Ford tempered his stand when the Nazis swarmed across the Continent in 1940. He despised war on moral grounds and cited George Washington's warning against foreign entanglements as justification. Although he became one of the most prolific armament producers in history, he converted his plowshares to swords only with great reluctance.

President Franklin Roosevelt believed war was coming and with it a need to bolster the nation's security. In May 1940 he called for an increase in aircraft production to 50,000 airplanes a year—roughly 20 times the increase in fleet size he'd asked for just one year earlier. Ford responded with the startling proclamation that "with the counsel of men like [Charles] Lindbergh and [Eddie] Rickenbacker and without meddling by government agencies, the Ford Motor Company could swing into a production of a thousand airplanes of a standard design a day." Edsel, the company's president, reminded skeptics that the Ford Motor Company had been an aircraft manufacturer from 1925 to 1933, though the old Tri-motor was hardly a model for modern airplanes. . . .

In January 1941, . . . Ford executives were invited to visit Consolidated Aircraft in San Diego, California, with the hope that Ford might expand its involvement in aircraft production. Henry Ford had made it clear he wasn't interested in working with any aviation company, but Edsel made the fateful journey anyway, accompanied by Ford manufacturing boss Charles Sorenson. . . .

Sorensen in particular was not impressed with the methods used to produce the new B-24 Liberator bomber. . . . [He] was convinced that precision-made wing sub-assemblies supplied by Ford would never fit—and he said so. When asked how he would manufacture the B-24, Sorensen replied confidently, "I'll have something for you tomorrow morning." . . .

By 4 a.m. his sums were in order. He estimated that it would take 100,000 workers and a $200 million plant measuring a mile long by a quarter-mile wide to deliver one finished airplane every hour. Sorensen knew that by using the same assembly line methods he had perfected in building more than 30 million Ford automobiles, it was feasible to eclipse Consolidated's modest goal of one airplane per day. . . .

Ford Motor Company had committed its resources to one of the grandest industrial undertakings in history: construction of the world's largest manufacturing plant to build aircraft using unprecedented methods. . . .

With little more than a letter of intent from the government specifying a gradual phase-in of operations . . . an army of Ford laborers set to work in a frenzy. Late in March

1941, 300 men with saws, axes, and bulldozers attacked the 100-acre woodlot where the [Willow Run] plant would be situated. . . .

Back in Dearborn, the inevitable conclusion was that Consolidated had never engineered the B-24 for high-volume production. Regardless of how Consolidated had been forming a part, Ford applied its own methods. Consolidated used "soft" tooling that was inexpensive and easily revised. Ford preferred steel dies for punching out aluminum parts and cast iron dies for forming operations instead of Consolidated's imprecise drop forges and rubber-covered dies. Instead of cutting out parts from metal sheets with saws or routers, Ford punched out parts with blanking dies. Rather than drilling rivet holes in stacked sheets, Ford pierced them during the blanking operation. Hundreds of holes were punched at once in some die-formed reinforcements, while a single stroke of a 500-ton press could punch 2,000 rivet holes in large sheets.

Nine hundred men and women worked seven days a week night and day to design the critical tooling. The first die was ordered four days before the first tree was felled at Willow Run, and more than 30,000 dies—equivalent to eight or nine car model changeovers—were ultimately required to manufacture the bomber's 1,225,000 parts, which were held together by 400,000 rivets.

On April 18, 1941, five weeks after receiving its initial $3.4 million contract for subassemblies, Ford broke ground for the plant. The first concrete footings were poured two days later. On May 1, a New York Central Railroad spur reached the site just as the first piece of steel was erected. The plant was dedicated on June 16, 1941, nine days before the concrete floor was poured. (Later in the month, the very first contract between the United Auto Workers and the Ford Motor Company was signed.) Tarpaulins protected the heavy machinery from the weather while the plant was being built around it. . . .

Ford's scheme depended on an efficient flow of materials from receiving docks to storage cribs to manufacturing and assembly areas. Finished subassemblies, each one precisely interchangeable with the next, were transported to successive assembly stations, by conveyor for small parts, or by overhead crane for more cumbersome pieces.

One of the more remarkable machines in the plant was a 70-foot-long fixture that held the center wing subassembly while mating surfaces and mounting pads were machined. It performed 87 operations in minutes, and the time to build a wing was reduced from 19 days to a matter of hours, a net reduction of more than 10,000 labor-hours per aircraft. Another Ford innovation was the use of seam or spot welding to replace riveting in certain locations. Some 15,000 rivets per airplane were eliminated, reducing weight and saving 35,000 hours of labor every month. . . .

Production began in November 1941, but 10 months passed before the first B-24 rolled off the line. People began calling the plant "Willit Run?," prompting Senator Harry Truman to undertake a special investigation.

Then the numbers began to mount: from a net output of 56 airplanes for all of 1942 (most of which were assembled by Consolidated and Douglas in Oklahoma and Texas plants) to 31 airplanes in January 1943 and 190 in June. Ford was still a long way from one airplane per hour and the Army's goal of 405 per month, later raised to 535 per month. But by January 1944 the company was building more B-24s than anyone else. . . . In March, the Willow Run plant produced 453 airplanes in 468 hours.

The changes surrounding the vortex of activity within Willow Run's walls were cataclysmic. Workers flooded in from all 48 states, Hawaii, Puerto Rico, Canada, and Latin America. Resourceful landlords collected double rent for many rooms: while one tenant worked, the other slept.

To relieve some of the strain, the Public Housing Administration erected an entire town—Willow Village—virtually overnight with dormitories for single workers and small houses for families. . . .

When the books were closed on the war effort, Ford's Willow Run bomber plant had logged an enviable record. During 1944, its peak year, the plant had produced 93 million pounds of airframes (a more revealing measure of productivity than units since airplane sizes differ) with fewer than 29,000 workers, not counting thousands more outside the plant, a feat that no other manufacturing facility even approached. Willow Run's output nearly equaled Japan's entire production that year and was approximately half that of each of the nations of Germany, Great Britain, and the Soviet Union. Ford's assembly line methods led to a remarkable drop in the delivered price for B-24s: from $238,000 each in 1942 to $137,000 in 1944. A total of 8,685 B-24s were built at Willow Run, including 1,894 knocked-down kits shipped to other plants for assembly. In the spring of 1945, the plant received an Army-Navy "E" citation for exceptional war work.

Document C

Novel Excerpt

(From John Dos Passos, *The Big Money*. Boston: Houghton Mifflin, 1937, pp. 50–54, 56–58.)

Note: Dos Passos wove interpretive representations of actual people's lives or events into his fiction. He borrowed terms like "newsreel" and "camera eye" from contemporary cinema and photojournalism to denote these episodes. His resulting novels present a complex portrait of the United States in the Roaring Twenties, capturing the extravagance and corruption that led to the 1929 collapse and the Great Depression.

He was the eldest son of an Irish immigrant who during the Civil War had married the daughter of a prosperous Pennsylvania Dutch farmer and settled down to farming near Dearborn in Wayne County, Michigan;
like plenty of other Americans, young Henry grew up hating the endless sogging through the mud about the chores, the hauling and pitching manure, the kerosene lamps to clean, the irk and sweat and solitude of the farm.

He was a slender, active youngster, a good skater, clever with his hands; what he liked was to tend the machinery and let the others do the heavy work. His mother had told him not to drink, smoke, gamble, or go into debt, and he never did. . . .

Henry Ford had ideas about other things than the designing of motors, carburetors, magnetos, jigs and fixtures, punches and dies; he had ideas about sales;
that the big money was in economical quantity production, quick turnover, cheap interchangeable easily replaced standardized parts;
it wasn't until 1909, after years of arguing with his partners, that Ford put out the first Model T. Henry Ford was right.

That season he sold more than ten thousand tin lizzies, ten years later he was selling almost a million a year. . . .

In 1913 they established the assemblyline at Ford's. That season the profits were something like twentyfive million dollars, but they had trouble in keeping the men on the job, machinists didn't seem to like it at Ford's. . . .

Henry Ford had ideas about other things than production.

He was the largest automobile manufacturer in the world; he paid high wages; maybe if the steady workers thought they were getting a cut (a very small cut) in the profits, it would give trained men an inducement to stick to their jobs,

wellpaid workers might save enough money to buy a tin lizzie; the first day Ford's announced that cleancut properlymarried American workers who wanted jobs had a chance to make five bucks a day (of course it turned out that there were strings to it; always there were strings to it) such an enormous crowd waited outside the Highland Park plant

all through the zero January night

that there was a riot when the gates were opened; cops broke heads, jobhunters threw bricks; property, Henry Ford's own property, was destroyed. The company dicks [police] had to turn on the firehose to beat back the crowd.

The American Plan; automotive prosperity seeping down from above; it turned out there were strings to it.

But that five dollars a day
paid to good, clean American workmen
who didn't drink or smoke cigarettes or read or think,
and who didn't commit adultery
and whose wives didn't take in boarders,
made America once more the [frontier] of the sweated workers of the world;
made all the tin lizzies and the automotive age, and incidentally,
made Henry Ford the automobileer, the admirer of Edison, the birdlover,
the great American of his time. . .

. . . [I]n 1922 Henry Ford sold one million three hundred and thirtytwo thousand two hundred and nine tin lizzies; he was the richest man in the world.

Good roads had followed the narrow ruts made in the mud by the Model T. The great automotive boom was on. At Ford's production was improving all the time; less waste, more spotters, strawbosses, stoolpigeons (fifteen minutes for lunch, three minutes to go to the toilet, the Taylorized* speedup everywhere, reachunder, adjustwasher, screwdown bolt, shove in cotterpin, reachunder, adjustwasher, screwdown bolt, reachunderadjustscrewdownreachunderadjust, until every ounce of life was sucked off into production and at night the workmen went home gray shaking husks). . . .

* Frederick Winslow Taylor developed time and motion studies to take some of the drudgery out of labor. In fact, his process of simplifying work into a series of efficent motions helped create the assembly-line method of production.

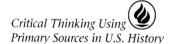

Critical Thinking Using
Primary Sources in U.S. History

New Era prosperity and the American Plan
(there were strings to it, always there were strings to it)
had killed Tin Lizzie.
Ford's was just one of many automobile plants.
When the stockmarket bubble burst,
Mr. Ford the crackerbarrel philosopher said jubilantly,
"I told you so.
Serves you right for gambling and getting in debt.
The country is sound."
But when the country on cracked shoes, in frayed trousers, belts tightened over hollow bellies,
idle hands cracked and chapped with the cold of that coldest March day of 1932,
started marching from Detroit to Dearborn, asking for work and the American Plan, all
they could think of at Ford's was machineguns.
The county was sound, but they mowed the marchers down.
They shot four of them dead.

Henry Ford as an old man
is a passionate antiquarian
(lives besieged in his father's farm embedded in an estate of thousands of millionaire acres,
protected by an army of servicemen, secretaries, secret agents, dicks under orders of an English
exprizefighter [Harry Bennett],
always afraid of the feet in broken shoes on the roads, afraid the gangs will kidnap his
grandchildren,
that a crank will shoot him,
that Change and the idle hands out of work will break through the gates and the high
fences;
protected by a private army against
the new America of starved children and hollow bellies and cracked shoes stamping on
souplines,
that has swallowed up the old thrifty farmlands
of Wayne County, Michigan, as if they had never been).

Document D

Nonfiction Extract

(From James K. Flink, *The Car Culture*. Cambridge: MIT Press, 1975, pp. 159–162.)

Mounting automobile registrations are undoubtedly the best indication that Americans in the 1920s continued to view automobility in balance as highly beneficial. . . .

Other data, however, indicate that for the bulk of the population the benefits of automobility, even by the early 1920s, were probably mainly symbolic. A questionnaire mailed by the National Automobile Chamber of Commerce in 1920 to a random sample of automobile owners in "ten widely selected states" showed scant evidence that automobility was improving the

Critical Thinking Using
Primary Sources in U.S. History

quality of car owners' lives. Of the owners who responded, 90 percent said their cars were "used more or less for business," and 60 percent of the mileage driven was "for business purposes." The NACC estimated a 57 percent "gain through car use over previous income or efficiency." . . . The most significant point was that only 37 percent of the owners reported "improving living conditions through use of the car (suburban life, etc.)," meaning that almost two-thirds of the automobile owners who responded found that the quality of their lives either had remained about the same or had deteriorated with automobility. . . .

The main things that automobility symbolized were material prosperity through a higher standard of living, individual mobility, and an improvement in the quality of life through a fusing of rural and urban advantages. If one excludes the obviously great payoff for such economic interest groups as the automobile and oil industries, real estate developers, and contractors, the realities of the automobile revolution fell far short of its proponents' promises for most Americans. As we have already seen, what the individual gained from automobile ownership was at the expense of undermining community and family, and it invited anonymity and anomie [rootlessness]. Improvements in the quality of life through a fusing of rural and urban advantages also proved illusory.

Reynold M. Wik's "grass-roots Americans" undoubtedly benefitted more than the urban masses from personal automobility. The motorcar and improved roads increased rural land values, lessened the drudgery of farm labor, ended rural isolation, and brought the farm family the amenities of city life, the most important being far better medical care and schools. In a day when "busing" has come to be associated in the minds of many Americans with an alleged lowering of educational standards, it seems particularly pertinent to point out that in the 1920s and 1930s the daily busing of farm children long distances to consolidated schools was hailed as a significant forward step in achieving educational parity between rural and urban schools.

These benefits of the school bus and the Model T notwithstanding, the cityward migration of farm youth was not stemmed, as auto enthusiasts promised it would be. Even more important, the family farm was already being killed off in the 1920s by a combination of the farm tractor, corporate agriculture, and the propensity of bankers to foreclose mortgages that had been incurred to finance the farmers' automobility. . . .

Proponents of automobility were right about the necessity of banishing the unsanitary horse from cities, and they were right that a viable urban transportation system could not run entirely on rails but also required great dependence on the more flexible motor vehicle. From the perspective of rational hindsight, however, the best solution to urban transportation problems would have been a balanced commitment to motortrucks and motor buses, along with rail transportation, rather than the mass ownership of private passenger cars in cities. By the 1920s it was obvious, contrary to the predictions of early proponents of automobility, that mass dependence on passenger cars had compounded urban traffic congestion and parking problems. Although it was not yet recognized, the urban neighborhood as a community was already being destroyed by the decentralization and segregation of activities encouraged by automobility and by the longer blocks, combined with widened streets and narrower sidewalks, that accommodation to the motorcar demanded. Nor was it foreseen that auto exhaust in the antiseptic, horseless city was going to prove even more detrimental to public health than horse exhaust once had been.

Contemporary Opinion

(From Jane Holtz Kay, *Asphalt Nation: How the Automobile Took Over America and How We Can Take It Back*. New York: Crown Publishers, 1997, pp. 191–194.)

. . . The great divide that separates post-1920s cities from their ancestors is the divide between a human-oriented world and car-oriented one. No more did a fan-ribbed pattern of settlement center around the vertical downtown or village cluster where the train or trolley stopped. Motorizing America limned [defined] the car-based sprawl to come. Not one city of "splendor" would surface after the 1920s launched America's "autohegemony."

In the neon city of downtown, streetcars still clanged. Despite the changing "riding habit," only 3 out of 120 cities lacked rail. Streetcars got more comfortable, their colors brightened. . . .

Street railway men were fighting for survival, however. Advertisements suggested their predicament. The traction operators' concern with "Making Transportation Pay" in a 1926 issue of a trade magazine became a more tremulous "Popularizing Public Transportation" and then the blatant "Selling Transportation." The chairman of Detroit's Rapid Transit complained, "We pay through delays and reduced efficiency. We pay through nervous wear and tear, through loss of property in blighted areas, and lessened values.". . . Subways, a long time in the making, won few new fans. And, as public transit showed its troubles and profits shrank, the railways sputtered along in red ink. "Bandits," the riders called the traction magnates, while the public asked, Why stand in line, why face the hurry-burly of strangers when the car promises comfort, privacy, and personal mobility? Demoralized, mass transit was caving. The steady parade of streetcars traveled on to extinction.

The mandate for wider roads and multilevel highways, spiralling to span some vast space with air-bound structures, revealed the expectation that the motor vehicle could control urban and technological reform to fashion a better world. . . . Reformers believed that inventions like the "freeway" were promising and would reduce the ever-growing menace to health from fumes. . . .

To motoring America, "fill 'er up" was indeed the national "have a nice day" by the decade's end. In 1928 consumerism seemed endless. Poverty looked as out of date as the horse and carriage, and America, as Herbert Hoover put it, was "bright with hope." Yet, the bargain was struck: automobility would replace all other forms of movement. In October 1929, Hoover's brightness dimmed, the feverish bull market went black, and hope crashed. Unbeknownst to those building for an unceasing tomorrow, the lights of the star city were flickering with that hope. The automobile had and would eclipse the past. "Changed. So changed," as *The Magnificent Ambersons* would conclude.

Commentary

(From Ivan Illich, Toward a History of Needs. New York: Random House, 1977, pp. 118–121.)

People move well on their feet. This primitive means of getting around will, on closer analysis, appear quite effective when compared with the lot of people in modern cities or on industrialized farms. It will appear particularly attractive once it has been understood that modern Americans walk, on the average, as many miles as their ancestors—most of them through tunnels, corridors, parking lots, and stores.

People on their feet are more or less equal. People solely dependent on their feet move on the spur of the moment, at three to four miles per hour, in any direction and to any place from which they are not legally or physically barred. An improvement on this native degree of mobility by new transport technology should be expected to safeguard these values and to add some new ones, such as greater range, time economies, comfort, or more opportunities for the disabled. So far this is not what has happened. Instead, the growth of the transportation industry has everywhere had the reverse effect. From the moment its machines could put more than a certain horsepower behind any one passenger, this industry has reduced equality among men, restricted their mobility to a system of industrially defined routes, and created time scarcity of unprecedented severity. As the speed of their vehicles crosses a threshold, citizens become transportation consumers on the daily loop that brings them back to their home, a circuit which the United States Department of Commerce calls a "trip" as opposed to the "travel" for which Americans leave home equipped with a toothbrush.

More energy fed into the transportation system means that more people move faster over a greater range in the course of every day. Everybody's daily radius expands at the expense of being able to drop in on an acquaintance or walk through the park on the way to work. Extremes of privilege are created at the cost of universal enslavement. An elite packs unlimited distance into a lifetime of pampered travel, while the majority spend a bigger slice of their existence on unwanted trips. . . .

What distinguishes the traffic in rich countries from the traffic in poor countries is not more mileage per hour of life-time for the majority, but more hours of compulsory consumption of high doses of energy, packaged and unequally distributed by the transportation industry.

Resources

Bibliography

Collier, Peter. *The Fords: An American Epic.* New York: Summit Books, 1987.

Finch, Christopher. *Highways to Heaven: The AUTO Biography of America.* New York: HarperCollins, 1992.

Flink, James J. *The Car Culture.* Cambridge: MIT Press, 1975.

Flink, James J. *The Automobile Age.* Cambridge: MIT Press, 1988.

Ford, Henry. *My Life and Work.* Cambridge, MA: Productivity Press, 1988. Reprint of 1922 edition.

Gelderman, Carol. *Henry Ford: The Wayward Capitalist.* New York: Dial Press, 1981.

Jardin, Anne. *The First Henry Ford: A Study in Personality and Business Leadership.* Cambridge: MIT Press, 1970.

Kay, Jane Holtz. *Asphalt Nation: How the Automobile Took Over America and How We Can Get It Back.* New York: Crown Publishers, 1997.

Lacey, Robert. *Ford, the Man and the Machine.* Boston: Little, Brown, 1986.

Lewis, David L., and Lawrence Goldstone, eds. *The Automobile and American Culture.* Ann Arbor: University of Michigan Press, 1993.

Sorensen, Charles. *My Forty Years with Ford.* New York: Norton, 1956.

Wik, Reynold. *Henry Ford and Grass-Roots America.* Ann Arbor: University of Michigan Press, 1972.

Media Resources

Documentaries

Birth of the Automobile. 47 minutes. WGBH, 1996. The first part of the video series *Driving Passion* made for Turner Network Television. Available from Teacher's Video, 800-262-8837.

Consuming Passions. 60 minutes. 1997. The first of the three-part PBS series *America on Wheels.* Available from Time-Life, Inc., 2000 Duke Street, Alexandria, VA 22314, 703-838-7000, or from Filmic Archives, Cinema Center, Botsford, CT 06404, 800-366-1920.

The Entrepreneurs: An American Adventure. 300 minutes. 1986. Contains an episode on Henry Ford. Available from Zenger Media, 800-421-4246.

Henry Ford. 50 minutes. 1994. Part of the Arts and Entertainment (A&E) series *Biography.* Available from Teacher's Video, 800-262-8837.

Henry Ford and the Mass Consumption Society. 29 minutes. 1981. Program 8 in the *American Business History* series. Available from the University of Minnesota.

Merrily We Roll Along. 54 minutes. NBC, 1961. A lighthearted Project XX social history of the automobile, narrated by Groucho Marx. Available from Zenger Media, 800-421-4246.

The Story of Henry Ford. 55 minutes. Questar Home Video. A program in the *Famous Americans of the 20th Century* series. Available from Teacher's Video, 800-262-8837.

Feature Films

Ford, the Man and the Machine. 200 minutes. 1987. A two-part television docudrama based on Robert Lacey's biography, it starred Cliff Robertson as Henry Ford. Available from Cabin Fever Entertainment, 203-863-5200.

UNIT 9

Elizabeth Gurley Flynn and the Radical Labor Movement

HISTORICAL BACKGROUND

Elizabeth Gurley Flynn was born in the small mill town of Manchester, New Hampshire, in 1890. As a child, she saw the poverty of the working class and the poor working conditions she had to endure. In 1900, her family moved to the Bronx in New York City, where they became active members of the Harlem Socialist Club. Her father was an organizer for the newly formed Industrial Workers of the World (IWW), also known as the "Wobblies." The IWW was different from other unions. It sought to organize workers by industry rather than skill level or job classification. It also had a political agenda—to usher in an era when organized labor would influence and eventually replace government. Flynn joined the IWW at the age of 16 and was soon active in IWW projects across the country. She was an effective and popular speaker and organizer.

Flynn became well known during the Lawrence, Massachusetts, mill strike in 1912. Along with "Big" Bill Haywood, she helped coordinate, or organize, the strike. During the strike, workers refused to work until owners met their demands. In Lawerence, the strike succeeded—workers won the higher pay they wanted. Confident of success, the IWW participated in the Paterson, New Jersey, strikes the next year. These ended in failure. In 1916, Flynn and another leader were expelled from the IWW. They advocated tactics not approved by union leadership during a strike by—and the arrests of—mine workers in the Mesabi range of Minnesota.

Word War I began in Europe in 1914, and for several years the United States remained neutral, providing no armed support for either side. As the United States prepared to join the fighting in 1917, the government supported a crackdown on the Wobblies for not backing the war. This governmental action and the failure of the Paterson strikes proved to be permanent setbacks for the IWW. Then, after World War I, a "Red Scare" followed the communist takeover of Russia durring the Bolshevik revolution. This scare, and renewed labor unrest at home, led to further suppression of labor and socialist organizations in the United States.

Flynn's commitment to her ideals remained unshaken. She joined the International Labor Defense in 1925 and continued her work on labor issues. She joined the American Communist Party in 1936, during the "Popular Front" era of the Depression. At that time, the Soviet Union was the only country actively opposed to fascist aggression in Spain and elsewhere. Thus, Americans opposed to fascism worked with American communists. She made speeches supporting communism and wrote articles for the communist newspaper, the *Daily Worker*. During World War II, she campaigned to secure rights for the many women who entered factories to support the war effort.

After the fighting stopped, an anticommunist reaction marked the start of the Cold War. Flynn became a target of early McCarthyism and the House Un-American Ac-

Critical Thinking Using
Primary Sources in U.S. History

tivities Committee. Joe McCarthy and the members of this committee were ready to accuse anyone with leftist ideals of being a subversive, a traitor. Flynn was arrested and imprisoned in 1951 on charges of plotting to overthrow the government. After her release from prison, Flynn continued her activities and was elected chair of the Communist Party of the USA (CPUSA).

In 1964, she won a court battle over the McCarran Act, which barred travel overseas by suspected subversives. This victory allowed her to travel to the Soviet Union, where she planned to write her autobiography. When she died of a stomach disorder later that year, she was given a full state funeral in Moscow's Red Square.

Key Questions About This Subject

- Against what economic and social injustices did Elizabeth Gurley Flynn fight during the early years of the twentieth century?
- Why did Flynn support the radical solutions offered by the Industrial Workers of the World and the Communist Party, and not the more gradual path adopted by the American Federation of Labor and other moderate unions?

- Did Flynn's advocacy of these changes, and of tactics to combat what she perceived as injustice, constitute "a clear and present danger"* to the United States government?"
- What role did popular hysteria play in these prosecutions?
- Under what circumstances should Americans' First Amendment rights be abridged and considered criminal behavior?

Mock Trial

If you are going to hold a simulated trial, here are the charges against Elizabeth Gurley Flynn (the Defendant): Elizabeth Gurley Flynn is accused of conspiring to overthrow the government of the United States through her activities, first as a Wobblie, and later as a Communist agitator. (Note that Flynn was actually tried for her work on behalf of the latter organization.)

* The "clear and present danger" test was adopted by the U.S. Supreme Court during the first "Red Scare" in 1919 to determine whether restraints on free speech could be justified. It was modified during the Cold War in 1950 to permit the gravity of the threat to offset a lack of immediacy.

Critical Thinking Using Primary Sources in U.S. History

Document A

"Sabotage: The Conscious Withdrawal of the Workers' Industrial Efficiency," 1915

(Transcribed from a speech Flynn gave during the Paterson strike of 1913. From FBI files, Aug. 15, 1949. NY, No. 100-1696, pp. 8–12.)

Its Necessity in the Class War

I am not going to attempt to justify sabotage on any moral ground. If the workers consider that sabotage is necessary, that in itself makes sabotage moral. Its necessity is its excuse for existence. . . . Sabotage is one weapon in the arsenal of labor to fight its side of the class struggle. Labor realizes, as it becomes more intelligent, that it must have power in order to accomplish anything; that neither appeals for sympathy nor abstract rights will make for better conditions. For instance, take an industrial establishment such as a silk mill where men and women and little children work ten hours a day for an average wage of between six and seven dollars a week. Could any one of them, or a committee representing the whole, hope to induce the employer to give better conditions by appealing to his sympathy, by telling him of the misery, the hardship and the poverty of their lives; or could they do it by appealing to his sense of justice? Suppose that an individual working man or woman went to an employer and said, "I make, in my capacity as wage worker in this factory, so many dollars' worth of wealth every day and justice demands that you give me at least half." The employer would probably have him removed to the nearest lunatic asylum. He would consider him too dangerous a criminal to let loose on the community! It is neither sympathy nor justice that makes an appeal to the employer. But it is power.

Short Pay, Less Work

. . . I have heard of my grandfather telling how an old fellow came to work on the railroad and the boss said, "Well, what can you do?"

"I can do 'most anything," said he—a big husky fellow.

"Well," said the boss, "can you handle a pick and a shovel?"

"Oh, sure. How much do you pay on this job?"

"A dollar a day."

"Is that all? Well,—all right. I need that job pretty bad. I guess I will take it." So he took his pick and went leisurely to work. Soon the boss came along and said:

"Say, can't you work any faster than that?"

"Shure I can."

"Well, why don't you?"

"This is my dollar-a-day clip."

"Well," said the boss, "let's see what the $1.25-a-day clip looks like."

That went a little better. Then the boss said, "Let's see what the $1.50-a-day clip looks like."

Critical Thinking Using
Primary Sources in U.S. History

The man showed him. "That was fine," said the boss, "well, maybe we will call it $1.50 a day." The man volunteered that his $2-a-day was a "hummer." So, through this instinctive sort of sabotage this poor obscure workingman on a railroad in Maine was able to gain for himself an advance from $1 to $2 a day. . . .

Interfering with Quality of Goods

The second form of sabotage is to deliberately interfere with the quality of the goods. And in this we learn many lessons from our employers, even as we learn how to limit the quantity. You know that every year in the western part of this United States there are fruits and grains produced that never find a market; bananas and oranges rot on the ground, whole skiffs of fruits are dumped into the ocean. Not because people do not need these foods and couldn't make good use of them in the big cities of the east, but because the employing class prefer to destroy a large percentage of the production in order to keep the price up in cities like New York, Chicago, Baltimore and Boston. . . . Yet if the worker attempts to apply the same principle, the same theory, the same tactic as his employer, we are confronted with all sorts of finespun moral objections.

Document B

Letter from Eugene V. Debs

(Written Feb. 1, 1926, paying tribute to Flynn)

Note: Debs was a prominent American labor leader and socialist candidate for the presidency several times during the early 1900s. For further information, please consult the "Witness List" in the Mock Trials section.

Ruth Albert, Executive Secretary League for Mutual Aid, New York City.

My dear Miss Albert:

Please allow me to thank you for your kindness in writing me in regard to the Dinner proposed to be given to our loyal and dearly beloved comrade, Elizabeth Gurley Flynn, on the fourteenth instant. The invitation to participate in the happy occasion honors me and is appreciated accordingly, and were it at all possible I should be happy indeed to present my personal compliments to the guest of honor and to mingle with the good comrades who will honor themselves in this very beautiful and fitting celebration.

Elizabeth Gurley Flynn holds a proud and enviable position in the American labor movement and yet she is one of the humblest and most unpretentious of its members. Ever since I first heard of this brave, dauntless leader of the working class she has been at the forefront, one of its most eloquent spokesmen and one of its most consecrated servants. She has espoused and championed the cause of the weakest, lowliest, most despised and persecuted, even when she stood almost alone, and in this she has never weakened or wavered a moment but faced and fought the enemy without fear and without reference to consequences to herself.

Elizabeth Gurley Flynn is a typical proletarian leader, an intrepid warrior of the social revolution, and after twenty years of singlehearted devotion and unflinching service to the cause she is loved and honored throughout the labor movement of the United States.

And so I gladly join as do also my wife and my brother and his wife in the loving and appreciative testimonial to Elizabeth Gurley Flynn, our faithful friend and our high-souled comrade, and with all cordial greetings to you all and wishing you a most joyous and inspiring celebration I am,

Yours Faithfully,
[Signed] Eugene V. Debs

Document C

Smith Act

(Title 18, Chapter 115: Treason, Sedition, and Subversive Activities [18 USCS & 2385] June 28, 1940.)

Note: The Smith Act has never been repealed. However, Supreme Court decisions since 1962 have sharply limited its definitions of prohibited acts and disallowed its use to restrict civil liberties. Thus, it has lost much of its effectiveness, as have many Cold War antisubversive laws.

Whoever knowingly or willfully advocates, abets, advises, or teaches the duty, necessity, desirability, or propriety of overthrowing or destroying the government of the United States or the government of any State, Territory, District or Possession thereof, or the government of any political subdivision therein, by force or violence, or by the assassination of any officer of any such government; or

Whoever, with intent to cause the overthrow or destruction of any such government, prints, publishes, edits, issues, circulates, sells, distributes, or publicly displays any written or printed matter advocating, advising, or teaching the duty, necessity, desirability, or propriety of overthrowing or destroying any government in the United States by force or violence, or attempts to do so; or

Whoever organizes or helps or attempts to organize any society, group, or assembly of persons, who teach, advocate, or encourage the overthrow or destruction of any such government by force or violence; or becomes or is a member of, or affiliates with, any such society, group, or assembly of persons, knowing the purposes thereof—

Shall be fined under this title or imprisoned not more than twenty years, or both, and shall be ineligible for employment by the United States or any department or agency thereof, for the five years next following his conviction.

If two or more persons conspire to commit any offense named in this section, each shall be fined under this title or imprisoned not more than twenty years, or both, and shall be ineligible for employment by the United States or any department or agency thereof, for the five years next following his conviction.

As used in this section, the terms "organizes" and "organize," with respect to any society, group, or assembly of persons, include the recruiting of new members, the forming of new units, and the regrouping or expansion of existing clubs, classes, and other units of such society, group, or assembly of persons.

Cross-Examination by Prosecution in Flynn Trial

(As reproduced in Helen C. Camp, *Iron in Her Soul: Elizabeth Gurley Flynn and the American Left.* Pullman: Washington State University Press, 1994, pp. 247–248.)

Q: Now at the time you executed this application card didn't you also agree to accept the program and statutes of the Communist International?

A: I don't recall if that was on the application card of the communist party.

Q: Let me ask you this, Miss Flynn, when you signed that application card did you advocate an armed struggle for the overthrow of the International bourgeoisies?

A: No, I certainly didn't. I joined the Communist Party of the United States of America for the interests of the American working class.

Q: Didn't you agree at the time you signed that application card to subordinate yourself to all the decisions of the Comintern?

A: Not to my knowledge, no.

Q: The Party at the time was known as the American section of the Communist International, was it not?

A: No. I always heard it referred to as the Communist party, Communist Labor Party. At one time it was the worker's party. I never heard it referred to as the American section of the communist international. Maybe I wasn't sufficiently informed.

Autobiographical Extract

(From Elizabeth Gurley Flynn, *The Alderson Story: My Life as a Political Prisoner.* New York: International Publishers, 1963, pp. 12–13.)

The atmosphere at that time was heavy with McCarthyism, the cold war, and the Korean war, which affected all Smith Act cases. Our arrests had immediately followed the Supreme Court decision which upheld the constitutionality of the Smith Act and rejected the appeal of this first group of leaders in what was called the Dennis Case. They had been arrested in 1945. William Foster and I were the only two of the Communist Party's National Board of 13 who were not involved in this trial. . . . As the only woman member of the Board I felt quite embarrassed and at a loss to explain why I was not arrested with my co-workers. I felt discriminated against by Uncle Sam!

Later during our trial it became evident that there was legal strategy behind the government's action. I had been purposely left out of the first case and held over for the second trial, as a link between these two groups of defendants, who were charged in the same alleged conspiracy. My presence apparently was calculated to help the government establish continuity of the conspiracy. It was called the Flynn Case, which did not mitigate my indignation against the whole legal chicanery. As soon as all defendants were free on bail we faced another difficulty. We were unable to secure lawyers to represent us. After defense counsel in the first case had been threatened with jail and disbarment, no one wanted to defend communists in a Foley Square trial—and we could hardly blame them.

Resources

Bibliography

Camp, Helen C. *Iron in Her Soul: Elizabeth Gurley Flynn and the American Left*. Pullman: Washington State University Press, 1994.

Dubovsky, Melvin. *We Shall Be All: A History of the Industrial Workers of the World*. Chicago: Quadrangle Books, 1969.

Flynn, Elizabeth G. *The Alderson Story: My Life as a Political Prisoner*. New York: International Publishers, 1963.

Flynn, Elizabeth. *Rebel Girl: An Autobiography: My First Life*. New York: International Publishers, 1973.

Flynn, Elizabeth. *Words on Fire: The Life and Writings of Elizabeth Gurley Flynn*. New Brunswick, NJ: Rutgers University Press, 1987.

Preston, William, Jr. *Aliens and Dissenters: Federal Suppression of Radicals, 1903–1933*. Cambridge: Harvard University Press, 1987.

Renshaw, Patrick. *The Wobblies: The Story of Syndicalism in the United States*. Garden City, NY: Doubleday, 1967.

Media Resources

Documentaries

Elizabeth Gurley Flynn: The Rebel Girl. 20 minutes. Berkeley: University of California Extension Center for Media and Independent Learning, 510-624-0460.

The Wobblies. 89 minutes. 1980. Available from First Run Films, 800-876-1710.

Dramatic Films on the Radicalization of Labor

Joe Hill. 114 minutes. 1971. A swedish fictionalized docudrama about the Wobblie leader who was hanged in 1915. Not currently available on video.

The Killing Floor. 118 minutes. 1985. Deals with Chicago meatpacking industry unrest during and after Word War I, when both labor and racial issues were at work. Available from Kino Video, 800-562-3330.

Matewan. 130 minutes. Orion Home Video, 1987. Based upon director John Sayles' novel *Union Dues*, it deals with a West Virginia coal strike in the early 1920s. Available in video stores.

The Molly Maguires. 123 minutes. 1970. Deals with labor unrest and suppression in the Pennsylvania coal mines in the 1870s. Available from Teacher's Video Company, 800-262-8837.

The Triangle Factory Fire Scandal. 100 minutes. 1979. A television film about the 1911 New York City sweatshop fire that cost 145 immigrant women garment workers their lives. Available from Artison Entertainment, 800-677-0789.

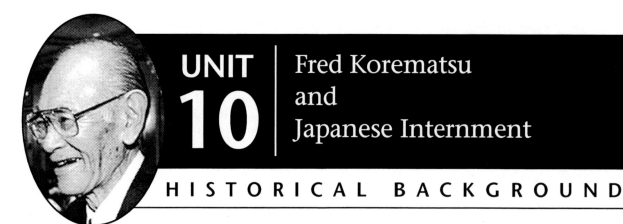

Fred Korematsu was born in 1919 in Oakland, California, with the given name Toyasoburo. His parents, who were immigrants from Japan, worked growing flowers for sale in San Francisco. Fred, as his American friends called him, worked in the greenhouses with them. Fred graduated from high school in 1938, and after struggling to make a living on his own, he returned to the family business for the next two years.

With the outbreak of war after the Japanese attack on Pearl Harbor, Fred tried to enlist in the U.S. Army; he was rejected due to his ancestry. Fred then took jobs as a welder, but was quickly fired from them, again due to his Japanese heritage. After President Roosevelt signed Executive Order 9066, General Dewitt began the mass removal of Japanese Americans from the west coast on the basis of the "threat" they posed to national security. The army ordered the Korematsu family to report to an internment camp, but Fred wished to remain with Ida Boitano, his fiancee. He made plans to leave California to avoid internment. While waiting to leave with Ida, he was arrested and charged with violating the order to evacuate.

After Ernest Besig, a lawyer with the ACLU (American Civil Liberties Union), posted his bail, the military police arrested him again. They brought him to the internment facility at Tanforan, where the rest of his family was located. Fred took his case to trial, but was found guilty of violating the order. He was sentenced to probation. This effectively returned him to Tanforan, as he planned to appeal the case to a higher court. While waiting for his appeal, Fred and other "disruptive" prisoners were moved to the Topaz camp, in a remote area of Nevada. After the appeals court denied his appeal, the ACLU took his case to the Supreme Court. By this time, 1944, *nisei*, Americans born to Japanese parents, were allowed to leave the camps to work. Fred left for Salt Lake City, and then Detroit. In December of 1944, the Supreme Court denied Fred's appeal, citing the military necessity of the evacuation order.

With the end of the war in late 1945, the detention centers were closed. Fred was married in 1946 to Kathryn Pearson, and they moved back to California in 1950. In 1982 an attorney named Peter Irons uncovered documents suggesting that the government had suppressed evidence that might have helped Fred in his case. They again brought the case before the district court in San Francisco, and the court exonerated Fred Korematsu in a 1984 decision.

Key Questions About This Subject

- Why were Americans of Japanese descent treated differently on the West Coast during World War II than Americans of German and Italian descent were treated on the East Coast?

- Under what, if any, circumstances is the government justified in abridging the due process rights of individual citizens?*

Mock Trial

If you are going to hold a simulated trial, here are the charges against Fred Korematsu (the Defendant): Fred (Toyasoburo) Korematsu is accused of violating Public Law 503, codifying Executive Order 9066 (the wartime exclusion act), providing for the removal of any or all civilians from designated military zones.

* Title II of the McCarran Internal Security Act of 1950 authorized the President, in the event of invasion, insurrection, or war, to declare an "internal security emergency" during which the attorney general could order the detention, without due process, of anyone deemed a potential threat. This act was never applied to any individuals, though camps for this purpose (including some originally for the Japanese internment) were maintained. The act was repealed in 1971.

D O C U M E N T S

Document A

Act of Congress

(From 56 Stat. 173, 18 U.S.C.A. 97a. Seventy-seventh Congress of the United States of America, January 5, 1942.)

An Act
To provide a penalty for violation of restrictions or orders with
respect to persons entering, remaining in, leaving, or committing any
act in military areas or zones.

Be it enacted by the Senate and House of Representatives of the United States of America in Congress assembled, That whoever shall enter, remain in, leave, or commit any act in any military area or military zone prescribed, under the authority of an Executive order of the President, by the Secretary of War, or by any military commander designated by the Secretary of War, contrary to the restrictions applicable to any such area or zone or contrary to the order of the Secretary of War or any such military commander, shall, if it appears that he knew or should have known of the existence and extent of the restrictions or order and that his act was in violation thereof, be guilty of a misdemeanor and upon conviction shall be liable to a fine of not to exceed $5,000 or to imprisonment for not more than one year, or both, for each offense.

Sam Rayburn
Speaker of the House of Representatives

Carter Glass
President of the Senate pro tempore

Franklin D. Roosevelt

Document B

Executive Order 9066

(Authorizing the Secretary of War to prescribe military areas.)

WHERE AS the successful prosecution of the war requires every possible protection against espionage and against sabotage to national-defense material, national-defense premises, and national-defense utilities as defined in section 4, Act of April 20,1918, 40 Stat. 533, as amended by the act of November 30, 1940, 54 Stat. 1220, and the Act of August 21, 1941, 55 Stat. 655 (U.S.C., Title 50, Sec. 104):

NOW, THEREFORE, by virtue of the authority vested in me as President of the United States, and Commander in Chief of the Army and Navy, I hereby authorize and direct the Secretary of War, and the Military Commanders whom he may from time to time designate, whenever he or any designated Commander deems such actions necessary or desirable, to prescribe military areas in such places and of such extent as he or the appropriate Military Commanders may determine, from which any or all persons may be excluded, and with such respect to which, the right of any person to enter, remain in, or leave shall be subject to whatever restrictions the Secretary of War or the appropriate Military Commander may impose in his discretion. The Secretary of War is hereby authorized to provide for residents of any such area who are excluded therefrom, such transportation, food, shelter, and other accommodations as may be necessary, in the judgement of the Secretary of War or the said Military Commander, and until other arrangements are made, to accomplish the purpose of this order. . . .

I hereby further authorize and direct all Executive Departments, independent establishments and other Federal Agencies, to assist the Secretary of War or the said Military Commanders in carrying out this Executive Order, including the furnishing of medical aid, hospitalization, food, clothing, transportation, use of land, shelter, and other supplies, equipment, utilities, facilities, and services . . .

This order shall not be construed as modifying or limiting in any way the authority heretofore granted under Executive Order No. 8972, dated December 12, 1941, nor shall it be construed as limiting or modifying the duty and responsibility of the Federal Bureau of Investigation, with respect to the investigation of alleged acts of sabotage or the duty and responsibility of the Attorney General and the Department of Justice under the Proclamations of December 7 and 8, 1941, prescribing regulations for the conduct and control of alien enemies, except as such duty and responsibility is superseded by the designation of military areas there under.

Franklin D. Roosevelt
February 19,1942

Document C

Civilian Exclusion Order No. 27

Headquarters Western Defense Command and Fourth Army Presidio of San Francisco, California, April 30, 1942.*

1. Pursuant to the provisions of Public Proclamations Nos. 1 and 2, this Headquarters, dated March 2, 1942, and March 16, 1942, respectively, it is hereby ordered that from and after 12 o'clock noon, P.W.T., of Thursday, May 7, 1942, all persons of Japanese ancestry, both alien and non-alien, be excluded from that portion of Military Area No. I described as follows:

   All of that portion of the County of Alameda, State of California, within that boundary beginning at the point at which the southerly limits of the City of Berkeley meet San Francisco Bay; thence easterly and following the southerly limits of said city to College Avenue; thence southerly on College Avenue to Broadway; thence southerly on Broadway to the southerly limits of the City of Oakland; thence following the limits of said city westerly and northerly, and following the shoreline of San Francisco Bay to the point of beginning.

2. A responsible member of each family, and each individual living alone, in the above described area will report between the hours of 8:00 A.M. and 5:00 P.M., Friday, May 1, 1942, or during the same hours on Saturday, May 2, 1942, to the Civil Control Station located at:
   530 Eighteenth Street
   Oakland, California.

3. Any person subject to this order who fails to comply with any of its provisions or with the provisions of published instructions pertaining hereto or who is found in the above area after

* Similar orders were issued in areas throughout the west coast of the United States.

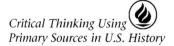

Critical Thinking Using
Primary Sources in U.S. History

12 o'clock noon, P.W.T., of Thursday, May 7, 1942 will be liable to the criminal penalties provided by Public Law No. 503, 77th Congress, approved March 21, 1942 entitled "An Act to Provide a Penalty for Violation of Restrictions or Orders with Respect to Persons Entering, Remaining in, Leaving, or Committing any Act in Military Areas or Zones," and alien Japanese will be subject to immediate apprehension and internment.

4. All persons within the bounds of an established Assembly Center pursuant to instructions from this Headquarters are excepted from the provisions of this order while those persons are in such Assembly Center.

> J.L. DeWitt
> Lieutenant General, U.S. Army
> Commanding

Document D

Internment Instructions

Western Defense Command and Fourth Army Wartime Civil Control Administration. Presidio of San Francisco, California. Instructions to all persons of Japanese Ancestry living in the following area:

All of that portion of the County of Alameda, State of California, within that boundary beginning at the point at which the southerly limits of the City of Berkeley meet San Francisco Bay; thence easterly and following the southerly limits of said city to College Avenue; thence southerly on College Avenue to Broadway; thence southerly on Broadway to the southerly limits of the City of Oakland; thence following the limits of said city westerly and northerly, and following the shoreline of San Francisco Bay to the point of beginning.

Pursuant to the provisions of Civilian Exclusion Order No. 27, this Headquarters, dated April 30, 1942, all persons of Japanese ancestry, both alien and non-alien, will be evacuated from the above area by 12 o'clock noon, P.W.T., Thursday May 7, 1942.

No Japanese person living in the above area will be permitted to change residence after 12 o'clock noon, P.W.T., Thursday, April 30, 1942, without obtaining special permission from the representative of the Commanding General, Northern California Sector, at the Civil Control Station located at:

530 Eighteenth Street,
Oakland, California.

Such permits will only be granted for the purpose of uniting members of a family, or in cases of grave emergency.

The Civil Control Station is equipped to assist the Japanese population affected by this evacuation in the following ways:

1. Give advice and instructions on the evacuation.
2. Provide services with respect to the management, leasing, sale, storage or other disposition of most kinds of property, such as real estate, business and professional equipment, household goods, boats, automobiles and livestock.
3. Provide temporary residence elsewhere for all Japanese in family groups.
4. Transport persons and a limited amount of clothing and equipment to their new residence.

Document E

Confidential War Office Memo

War Relocation Authority
Washington

August 12,1942

RELOCATION AND THE CONSTITUTION

Prepared by the Office of the Solicitor and the Office of
Reports for use of the War Relocation Authority Staff

Confidential   Confidential   Confidential

_____

When Uncle Sam last March ordered 112,000 people of Japanese ancestry to pack up and move out of military areas on the Pacific coast his action generated a storm of discussion and raises some legal questions of fundamental importance to the American people.

It was the first time in the history of the United States that anything like that had ever been done. True, the military dictators of Europe could have taken such action with no questions asked, but in a democracy—well, that was a different matter.

In the first place, two-thirds of the Japanese people in this country were born here and are therefore citizens—with the same rights as any of the rest of us. Where then, did the Federal Government get its legal authority to uproot a whole people and transplant them? What basis could be found in the Constitution for such action? Did it mean that the Bill of Rights was also to be scrapped for the duration?

There is no pat answer for these questions nor can they be considered from the standpoint of what would have been right and just ten years ago, or even one year ago when this country was not at war. They must be considered against the backdrop of total war, and from the standpoint of a nation fighting for its existence. . . .

*Critical Thinking Using
Primary Sources in U.S. History*

The main constitutional problem centers around detaining American citizens of Japanese ancestry. Under sweeping war-time powers, the Federal Government can order the detention, or place other restriction upon ANY citizen—so long as such restrictions are justified, reasonable and necessary in the protection of national safety and in the preservation of national existence. That does not mean, however, the Government can set aside the Bill of Rights to suit its convenience. Every citizen still has redress to the courts. Every citizen still retains the rights guaranteed him by the Bill of Rights—but those rights may be curtailed in time of war to protect the national safety.

So the constitutional question simmers down to this: Can it be shown that the detention of citizen-Japanese at relocation centers is a reasonable and necessary step for the protection of national safety?

How the courts will answer that question is as yet undetermined, but here, in broad outline, are the defense positions the Federal Government will take in the event the legality of its evacuation and relocation program is challenged:

The action taken with respect to Japanese in this country is justifiable on the grounds of military necessity for several reasons.

1. All Japanese look very much alike to a white person—it is hard for us to distinguish between them. It would be hard to tell a Japanese soldier in disguise from a resident Japanese. The danger of infiltration by Japanese parachutists, soldiers, etc. is, therefore, reduced and the chances of detecting any attempt at infiltration are increased.

2. The Japanese Government has always tried to maintain close ties with and control over Japanese people in this country with the result that many of them have never really been absorbed into American life and culture. Many Japanese-Americans have been educated in Japan. Many, believers in Shintoism, worship the Emperor and regard his orders as superior to any loyalty they may owe the United States. Therefore, the action has reduced the danger of successful invasion by removing an element of the population which had never been assimilated and which might not successfully withstand the strong emotional impulse to change loyalties or give way to their true feelings in the event that Japanese troops should land on our shores.

3. Evacuation and limited detention of the Japanese is justified as a measure in the prevention of sabotage and fifth-column* activities. We know that there is a Japanese fifth-column in this country but nobody knows who is in it or how large it is. Some members of it have been caught and, after a hearing, interned. Since it is impossible for us to distinguish between the loyal and the disloyal Japanese, we may avoid the danger of fifth-column activity, sabotage and espionage by removing all Japanese from the danger zones and detaining them in other places.

4. In time of war the judgment of the military authorities is entitled to great weight and should not be lightly pushed aside. Since they have decided that evacuation and detention of the Japanese is a necessary precaution in fighting this war their judgment should stand unless it is proved wrong.

5. The action taken was reasonable and necessary for the protection of the Japanese themselves. It minimized the dangers of mob violence and local disorders growing out of war hysteria and racial discrimination. Through lessening the possibility of harsh treatment of

---

* Relating to a group of citizens or residents of the country who are enemy sympathizers engaging in spying or sabotage within national borders.

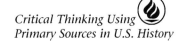

Critical Thinking Using
Primary Sources in U.S. History

Japanese in this country (incidents which would have been exploited promptly by Axis propagandists who wish to make it appear to be a race war) it took away an excuse for even harsher retaliatory treatment of American prisoners by Japan.

Since its creation by Executive Order of the President on March 18, 1942, as the agency charged with the responsibility of relocating the Japanese after their evacuation, the War Relocation Authority has taken steps to strengthen its position on the constitutional question by the adoption of administrative procedures to relax regulations and permit citizen-Japanese to leave relocation centers to accept employment under certain specified conditions. These procedures will change an absolute detention into a qualified detention and will therefore strengthen the reasonableness of the action.

Document F

Personal Narrative

Chieko Hirata [Teacher]
Period II, English I

My Last Day At Home

The month of May when I was attending school, all the residents of Hood River county, as well as the people of the whole western coast was surprised to receive such an unexpected order of evacuation.

Promptly after hearing about the order I with my folks went to register and then for a brief physical examination. Then I helped my folks pack and prepared to leave my dear home on May 13, 1942.

On May 8, 1942 I withdrew from Parkdale Grade School, where all my friends and teachers bid me farewell with sorrowful face and tears. Our packing never seem to cease, we kept on packing then finally we were finished. Then came May 13th, my most dreaded day which I shall never forget the rest of my life. On the afternoon of the 13th, I board the train headed for Pinedale, California.

On the night of the 15th we arrived. The weather was pretty hot. In Pinedale I lived in the D-section which had forty barracks, which had [five] apartments to a barrack.

I stayed at the Pinedale Assembly Center about two months. Then around July 15, 1942 we received our order to evacuate for Tule Lake. Then on July 18th we evacuated for Tule Lake and spent a night on the train. I arrived in Tule Lake. At present I am living in Block 58. The residents of this block is most Tacoma folks which I am not very much acquainted with as yet. Being that my cousin lives in Block 57 I am always visiting them.

I am always hoping that this war will end, so that I will be able to go back to Parkdale, my home town and see all my old friends, and live to my dying days in my old home in Parkdale, Oregon.

—Herbert Yoshikawa [Student Author]

Hirabayashi v. *United States*, 320 U.S. 81, 1943

Hir[a]bayashi, an American citizen of Japanese ancestry, was convicted in the district court of knowingly disregarding restrictions made applicable by a military commander to persons in a military area prescribed by him as such, all as authorized by an Executive Order of the President. The questions before the court was whether the particular restriction violated, namely that all persons of Japanese ancestry residing in such an area be within their place of residence daily between the hours of 8:00 p.m. and 6:00 a.m., was adopted by the military commander in the exercise of an unconstitutional delegation by Congress of its legislative power, and whether the restriction unconstitutionally discriminated between citizens of Japanese ancestry and those of other ancestries in violation of the Fifth Amendment. . . . There is support for the view that social, economic and political conditions which have prevailed since the close of the last century, when the Japanese began to come to this country in substantial numbers, have intensified their solidarity and have in large measure prevented their assimilation as an integral part of the white population. . . . Congress and the Executive, including the military commander, could have attributed special significance, in its bearing on the loyalties of persons of Japanese descent, to the maintenance by Japan of its system of dual citizenship. . . . The restrictions, both practical and legal, affecting the privileges and opportunities afforded to persons of Japanese extraction residing in the United States, have been sources of irritation and may well have tended to increase their isolation, and in many instances their attachments to Japan and its institutions.

Viewing these data in all their aspects, Congress and the Executive could reasonably have concluded that these conditions have encouraged the continued attachment of members of this group to Japan and Japanese institutions. . . . We cannot say that the war-making branches of the Government did not have ground for believing that in a critical hour such persons could not readily be isolated and separately dealt with, and constituted a menace to the national defense and safety, which demanded that prompt and adequate measures be taken to guard against it. . . . Distinctions between citizens solely because of their ancestry are by their very nature odious to a free people whose institutions are founded upon the doctrine of equality. For that reason, legislative classification or discrimination based on race alone has often been held to be a denial of equal protection. . . . We may assume that these considerations would be controlling here were it not for the fact that the danger of espionage and sabotage, in time of war and of threatened invasion, calls upon the military authorities to scrutinize every relevant fact bearing on the loyalty of populations in the danger areas. . . . The adoption by Government, in the crisis of war and of threatened invasion, of measures for the public safety, based upon the recognition of facts and circumstances which indicate that a group of one national extraction may menace that safety more than others, is not wholly beyond the limits of the Constitution and is not to be condemned merely because in other and in most circumstances racial distinctions are irrelevant. . . .What we have said also disposes of the contention that the curfew order involved an unlawful delegation by Congress of its legislative power. . . . Affirmed.

88 *Critical Thinking Using*
Primary Sources in U.S. History

Yasui v. *United States*, 320 U.S. 115, 1943

Yasui, an American-born person of Japanese ancestry, was convicted in the district court of an offense of a curfew order. Evidence presented at trial showed that Yasui was born in Oregon in 1916 of alien parents; when he was eight years old he spent a summer in Japan; he attended the public schools in Oregon, and also, for about three years, a Japanese language school; he later attended the University of Oregon, from which he received A.B and LL.B degrees; he was a member of the bar of Oregon, and a second lieutenant in the Army of the United States, Infantry Reserve; he had been employed by the Japanese Consulate in Chicago, but had resigned on December 8, 1941, and immediately offered his services to the military authorities; he had discussed with an agent of the Federal Bureau of Investigation the advisability of testing the constitutionality of the curfew; and that when he violated the curfew order he requested that he be arrested so that he could test its constitutionality.

. . . [We] hold, as in the Hirabayashi case, that the curfew order was valid as applied to citizens. . . . and the conviction must be sustained. . . . But as the sentence of one year's imprisonment—the maximum permitted by the state—was imposed after the finding that appellant was not a citizen, and as the Government states that it has not and does not now controvert his citizenship, the case is an appropriate one for resentence in the light of these circumstances. . . . The conviction will be sustained but the judgment will be vacated and the cause remanded to the district court for resentence . . . and to afford that court opportunity to strike its findings as to appellant's loss of United States citizenship.

Endo, Ex Parte 323, U.S. 283, 1944

Mitsuye Endo, an American citizen, had been granted leave clearance by the War Relocation Authority, but the Western Defense Command would not allow her to re-enter the restricted zone. The Supreme Court, the Court ruled that a loyal American citizen could not be held in a relocation camp against her will.

A citizen who is concededly loyal presents no problem of espionage or sabotage. Loyalty is a matter of the heart and mind not of race, creed, or color. He who is loyal is by definition not a spy or a saboteur. When the power to detain is derived from the power to protect the war effort against espionage and sabotage, detention which has no relationship to that objective is unauthorized.

Nor may the power to detain an admittedly loyal citizen or to grant him a conditional release be implied as a useful or convenient step in the evacuation program, whatever authority might be implied in case of those whose loyalty was not conceded or established. If we assume (as we do) that the original evacuation was justified, its lawful character was derived from the fact that it was an espionage and sabotage measure, not that there was community hostility to this group of American citizens. The evacuation program rested explicitly on the former ground not on the latter as the underlying legislation shows. The authority to detain a citizen or to grant him a conditional release as protection against espionage or sabotage is exhausted at least when his loyalty is conceded. . . . Community hostility even to loyal evacuees may have been (and perhaps still is) a serious problem. But if authority for their custody and supervision is to be sought on that ground, the Act of March 21, 1942, offer no support. And none other is advanced. To read them that broadly would be to assume that the Congress and the President intended that this discriminatory action should be taken against these people wholly on account of their ancestry even though the government conceded their loyalty to this country. We cannot make such an assumption. As the President has said of these loyal citizens: 'Americans of Japanese ancestry, like those of many other ancestries, have shown that they can, and want to, accept our institutions and work loyally with the rest of us, making their own valuable contribution to the national wealth and well-being. In vindication of the very ideals for which we are fighting this war it is important to us to maintain a high standard of fair, considerate, and equal treatment for the people of this minority as of all other minorities.' Mitsuye Endo is entitled to an unconditional release by the War Relocation Authority.

Document J

Korematsu v. *United States*, 323 U.S. 214, 1944

Fred Korematsu was arrested and convicted for not reporting to an assembly center in May 1942 . . . was convicted in a federal district court for remaining in San Leandro, California, a 'Military Area,' contrary to Civilian Exclusion Order No. 34 of the Commanding General [323 U.S. 214, 216] of the Western Command, U.S. Army, which directed that after May 9, 1942, all persons of Japanese ancestry should be excluded from that area. No question was raised as to petitioner's loyalty to the United States. . . . It should be noted, to begin with, that all legal restrictions which curtail the civil rights of a single racial group are immediately suspect. That is not to say that all such restrictions are unconstitutional. It is to say that courts must subject them to the most rigid scrutiny. Pressing public necessity may sometimes justify the existence of such restrictions; racial antagonism never can. . . . In the light of the principles we announced in the Hirabayashi case, we are unable to conclude that it was beyond the war power of Congress and the Executive to exclude those of Japanese ancestry from the West Coast war area at the time they did. . . . They did so, as pointed out in our Hirabayashi opinion, in accordance with Congressional authority to the military to say who should, and who should not, remain in the threatened areas. Here, as in the Hirabayashi case, . . . we cannot reject as unfounded the judgment of the military authorities and of Congress that there were disloyal members of that population, whose number and strength could not be precisely and quickly ascertained. . . . [We] uphold the exclusion order as of the time it was made and when the petitioner violated it. . . . It is said that we are dealing here with the case of imprisonment of a citizen in a concentration camp solely because of his ancestry, without evidence or inquiry concerning his loyalty and good disposition towards the United States. Our task would be simple, our duty clear, were this a case involving the imprisonment of a loyal citizen in a concentration camp because of racial prejudice. Regardless of the true nature of the assembly and relocation centers—and we deem it unjustifiable to call them concentration camps with all the ugly connotations that term implies—we are dealing specifically with nothing but an exclusion order. To cast this case into outlines of racial prejudice, without reference to the real military dangers which were presented, merely confuses the issue. Korematsu was not excluded from the Military Area because of hostility to him or his race. He was excluded because we are at war with the Japanese Empire, because the properly constituted military authorities feared an invasion of our West Coast and felt constrained to take proper security measures, because they decided that the military urgency of the situation demanded that all citizens of Japanese ancestry be segregated from the West Coast temporarily, and finally, because Congress, reposing its confidence in this time of war in our military leaders—as inevitably it must—determined that they should have the power to do just this. There was evidence of disloyalty on the part of some, the military authorities considered that the need for action was great, and time was short. We cannot—by availing ourselves of the calm perspective of hindsight—now say that at that time these actions were unjustified. Affirmed.

Document K

Civil Liberties Act of 1988

(From "Restitution for World War II Internment of Japanese-Americans and Aleuts," 50 App. USCA s 1989, Pub. L. 100-383, Sec. 1, August 10, 1988, 102 Stat. 903.)

The purpose of this Act (sections 1989 to 1989d of this Appendix) are to—

(1) acknowledge the fundamental injustice of the evacuation, relocation, and internment of United States citizens and permanent resident aliens of Japanese ancestry during World War II;

(2) apologize on behalf of the people of the United States for the evacuation, relocation, and internment of such citizens and permanent resident aliens;

(3) provide for a public education fund to finance efforts to inform the public about the internment of such individuals so as to prevent the recurrence of any similar event;

(4) make restitution to those individuals of Japanese ancestry who were interned;

(5) make restitution to Aleut residents of the Pribilof Islands and the Aleutian Islands west of Unimak Island, in settlement of United States obligations in equity and at law, for—

   (A) injustices suffered and unreasonable hardships endured while those Aleut residents were under United States control during World War II;

   (B) personal property taken or destroyed by United States forces during World War II;

   (C) community property, including community church property, taken or destroyed by United States forces during World War II; and

   (D) traditional village lands on Attu Island not rehabilitated after World War II for Aleut occupation or other productive use;

(6) discourage the occurrence of similar injustices and violations of civil liberties in the future; and

(7) make more credible and sincere any declaration of concern by the United States over violations of human rights committed by other nations.

Resources

Bibliography

Armor, John, and Peter Wright. *Manzanar*. New York: Random House, 1988.

Bosworth, Allan R. *America's Concentration Camps*. New York: W.W. Norton, 1967.

Daniels, Roger, ed. *American Concentration Camps*. New York: Garland, 1989. 9 volumes.

Daniels, Roger. *Concentration Camps: North American Japanese in the United States and Canada During World War II*. Melbourne, FL: Kreiger, 1993.

Daniels, Roger. *The Decision to Relocate the Japanese Americans*. Melbourne, FL: Krieger, 1985.

Daniels, Roger. *The Politics of Prejudice: The Anti-Japanese Movement in California and the Struggle for Japanese Exclusion*. Berkeley: University of California Press, 1978.

Irons, Peter. *Justice at War: The Story of the Japanese-American Internment Cases*. New York: Oxford University Press, 1983.

Irons, Peter, ed. *Justice Delayed: The Record of the Japanese American Internment Cases*. Middleton, CT: Wesleyan University Press, 1989.

Levine, Ellen. *A Fence Away from Freedom: Japanese Americans and World War II*. New York: Putnam, 1985.

Maki, Mitchell T., Harry H.L. Kitano, and S. Megan Berthhold. *Achieving the Impossible Dream: How Japanese Americans Obtained Redress*. Urbana and Chicago: University of Illinois Press, 1999.

Nishimoto, Richard, and Dorothy Thomas. *The Spoilage: Japanese-American Evacuation and Resettlement During World War II*. Berkeley: University of California Press, 1969.

Report of the Commission on Wartime Relocation and Internment of Civilians. *Personal Justice Denied*. Washington DC: U.S. Government Printing Office, 1982. A summary of this report and a "Photo Aid" set are available from Social Studies School Service, 800-421-4246.

Takaki, Ronald. *Double Victory: A Multicultural History of America in World War II*. Boston: Little, Brown and Company, 2000.

Media Resources

Documentaries

Guilty by Reason of Race. 52 minutes. NBC News, 1972. An early examination of the internment made at the time of the first reawakening of interest in the issue. Not currently available.

The Japanese American Internment: Lessons for American Society. 60 minutes. U.S. State Department, 1996. Based on a discussion of his family's experiences by Congressman Robert Matsui.

Japanese Relocation. 10 minutes. 1942. The official and self-congratulatory justification of Japanese internment. Available from Zenger Media, 800-421-4246.

Nisei Soldier: Standard Bearer for an Exiled People. 30 minutes. 1984. And *The Color of Honor: The Japanese American Soldier in World War II*. 90 minutes. 1989. Trace the service of Japanese-American soldiers during World War II in such units as the 442nd Regimental Combat Team, the most highly decorated unit of the U.S. Army, whose motto was "Go for Broke," while many of their families were interned. Both available from Vox Production, 415-673-642, or from the Japanese American National Museum, 800-461-5266.

Something Strong Within. 40 minutes. A film about life in the relocation camps using home movies shot there by the detainees. Made for the Japanese American National Museum. Available from Zenger Media, 800-421-4246.

A Time Remembered: The Terminal Island Story. 42 minutes. Traces the story of the Japanese-American fishing community in Los Angeles Harbor and the impact of the relocation on it. Available from Zenger Media, 800-421-4246.

Unfinished Business: The Japanese American Internment Cases. 60 minutes. Farallon Films, 1985. Tells the stories of the three Japanese Americans who decided to take their cases to the Supreme Court: Fred Korematsu, Gordon Hirabayashi, and Minoru Yasui. Available from National Asian American Telecommunications Association, 415-552-9550.

Educational Media

Executive Order 9066: The Incarceration of Japanese Americans During World War II. CD-ROM for Windows. Produced in 1988 by the Japanese American National Museum, the UCLA Film and Television Archive, and Mitsui (USA). Available from the Japanese American National Museum, 800-461-5266.

Dramatic Films

Come See the Paradise. 133 minutes. 1990. Alan Parker's film about internment. It has an "R" rating. Available from Movies Unlimited, 800-466-8437.

Farewell to Manzanar. 105 minutes. 1976. The dramatic television film about one family's internment, based upon the autobiographical book by Jeanne Wakatuski and her husband James D. Houston (they also wrote the screenplay). Not currently available on video, but the book and a reproducible unit based on it are available from Social Studies School Service, 800-421-4246.

Go for Broke. 91 minutes. 1951. Traces the transformation of an American officer (played by Van Johnson) who is put in charge of a Japanese-American army unit early in World War II. Available from Teacher's Video Company, 800-262-8837.

Midway. 132 minutes. 1976. One of the subplots concerns an American flyer in love with a Japanese American whose family was interned on Sand Island, near Honolulu. Available at many video stores.

1941. 120 minutes. 1979. Deals with the hysteria that broke out in Los Angeles in the wake of the Pearl Harbor bombing. It is a black comedy based on a real incident that took place in December 1941. Available from Critics Choice Video, 800-367-7765.

Snow Falling on Cedars. 130 minutes. 2000. Based on David Guterson's novel, the movie tells the story of a Japanese-American fisherman, falsely accused of murder on San Pedro Island in Puget Sound. The atmosphere of the 1954 trial is affected by memories (told in flashbacks) of the period of WWII exclusion. Available on video from Facets Multimedia, 800-331-6197.

The War Between Us. 108 minutes. 1995. A Lifetime Cable Television movie about the Japanese-Canadian internment in British Columbia. Not currently available on video.

UNIT 11 | Harry S. Truman and the Dropping of the Atomic Bomb

HISTORICAL BACKGROUND

Harry Truman was born in Missouri in 1884 and grew up in the town of Independence, close to Kansas City. After taking over the family farm in 1906, Truman became active in local politics. He was an active member of the local Democratic party, as well as the local farm federation, the Masons, and the National Guard. Called to active service during World War I, Truman served as an officer of artillery on the Western front. Returning home to Missouri, he was a partner in a clothing store that soon failed. He then entered politics, sponsored by "Boss" Thomas J. Pendergast's Kansas City political machine.

After holding several county level offices, Truman was elected to the U.S. Senate, where he was an active supporter of Franklin Roosevelt's New Deal programs. Winning a close reelection in 1940, Truman became chairman of a Senate committee on waste and inefficiency in military production during World War II. Its investigations brought Truman national attention. Popular in the Democratic party, Truman was selected to replace Henry Wallace as Roosevelt's running mate in 1944. After Roosevelt's death in April 1945, Truman became president.

Truman was faced with the end of the war, including the surrender of Germany in May of 1945. After taking office, he was informed of the atomic bomb program. Once the bomb had been tested successfully, he authorized the use of atomic bombs on Hiroshima and Nagasaki, hoping to end the war without having to invade Japan. The bombs were dropped on August 6 (Hiroshima) and August 9 (Nagasaki). Most, though not all, American soldiers awaiting invasion orders believed then—and still believe now—that the bombs saved their lives. Others suggest that a combination of events may have forced the Japanese surrender: the bombings, the continuing Allied blockade, the quiet dropping of an American demand to include the emperor's abdication in an unconditional surrender, and the vanishing of Japan's last hope for a negotiated settlement when the Soviet Union entered the Pacific war on August 8, between the bombings of Hiroshima and Nagasaki.

The war over, Truman dedicated himself to halting the expansion of Soviet power, implementing the Marshall Plan, and building the NATO treaty.

Winning a close second-term election in 1948 over Thomas Dewey, Truman faced the loss of China to the communists, the growing "red hunt" at home, and increasing agitation over his civil rights and "Fair Deal" programs. The outbreak of the Korean War proved difficult for Truman, with its early setbacks and a growing conflict with General MacArthur that resulted in his dismissal of MacArthur. In 1952 Truman declined to run for president again. Harry Truman died in 1972.

Key Questions About This Subject

- What reasons were given for dropping atomic bombs on Japan at the time? What reasons were given later?*
- What role in the decision to use atomic bombs did recent American casualties play: nearly 26,000 casualties (including 6,821 dead) to capture Iwo Jima in February and March 1945; and 49,151 casualties (including 12,520 dead) on Okinawa between April and July 1945?
- What arguments did the Franck Report give concerning the use of the bombs?
- What alternatives were available?

- What role did concerns about the Soviet Union play in the decision?
- Did victims of atomic bombings suffer a significantly different impact from the destruction caused by fire bombings elsewhere in Japan, such as the Great Tokyo Air Raid of March 9–10, 1945, when 279 B-29s dropped 1,665 tons of napalm incendiary bombs on the city, which burned 16 square miles of the city to the ground, destroying the homes of over a million residents, killing 83,793 people, and injuring 41,000 more? If so, how?

Mock Trial

If you are going to hold a simulated trial, here are the charges against Harry S. Truman (the Defendant): Harry S. Truman, president of the United States, is accused of war crimes as a result of his decision to use the atomic bombs on the cities of Hiroshima and Nagasaki, resulting in the deaths of more than 100,000 Japanese civilians and the exposure of many times that number to the effects of nuclear radiation.

* Some have argued that race played a role in the decision to use on Japan a bomb originally designed to deter Nazis from using one they were developing. Some believed at the time that the bombs were just retribution for the sneak attack on Pearl Harbor. It has also been suggested that technical (two different kinds of bombs were used over the Japanese cities) or political considerations may have played a role. General Groves suggested that if the bombs weren't used as soon as they were available, political campaigns would subsequently be fought over how many American lives were needlessly lost because of the delay or over how much government money was squandered on this untested boondoggle.

Document A

Memo Discussed by Secretary of War Stimson and General Groves with Truman, April 25, 1945

(From Michael B. Stoff, Jonathan F. Fanton, and R. Hal Williams, eds., *The Manhattan Project: A Documentary Introduction to the Atomic Age.* New York: McGraw Hill Inc., 1991, pp. 95–96.)

1. Within four months we shall in all probability have completed the most terrible weapon ever known in human history, one bomb of which could destroy a whole city.

2. Although we have shared its development with the UK, physically the US is at present in the position of controlling the resources with which to construct and use it and no other nation could reach this position for some years.

3. Nevertheless it is practically certain that we could not remain in this position indefinitely.

    (a) Various segments of its discovery and production are widely known among many scientists in many countries, although few scientists are now acquainted with the whole process which we have developed.

    (b) Although its construction under present methods requires great scientific and industrial effort and raw materials, which are temporarily mainly within the possession and knowledge of US and UK, it is extremely probable that . . . the future will make it possible to be constructed by smaller nations or even groups, or at least by a large nation in a much shorter time.

4. As a result, it is indicated that the future may see a time when such a weapon may be constructed in secret and used suddenly and effectively with devastating power by a wilful nation or group against an unsuspecting nation or group of much greater size and material power. With its aid even a very powerful unsuspecting nation might be conquered within a very few days by a very much smaller one, although probably the only nation which could enter into production within the next few years is Russia.

5. The world in its present state of moral advancement compared with its technical development would be eventually at the mercy of such a weapon. In other words, modern civilization might be completely destroyed.

6. To approach any world peace organization of any pattern now likely to be considered, without an appreciation by the leaders of our country of the power of this new weapon, would seem to be unrealistic. No system of control heretofore considered would be adequate to control this menace. . . .

7. Furthermore, in the light of our present position with reference to this weapon, the question of sharing it with other nations and, if so shared, upon what terms, becomes a primary question of our foreign relations. Also our leadership in the war and in the development of this weapon has placed a certain moral responsibility upon us which we cannot shirk without very serious responsibility for any disaster to civilization which it would further.

8. On the other hand, if the problem of the proper use of this weapon can be solved, we would have the opportunity to bring the world into a pattern in which the peace of the world and our civilization can be saved.

9. As stated in General Groves' report, steps are under way looking towards the establishment of a select committee . . . for recommending action to the Executive and Legislative branches of our government when secrecy is no longer in full effect. . . . All recommendations would of course be first submitted to the President.

The Franck Report, June 11, 1945

. . . In the past, science has often been able to provide also new methods of protection against new weapons of aggression it made possible, but it cannot promise such efficient protection against the destructive use of nuclear power. This protection can come only from the political organization of the world. Among all the arguments calling for an efficient international organization for peace, the existence of nuclear weapons is the most compelling one. *In the absence of an international authority which would make all resort to force in international conflicts impossible, nations could still be diverted from a path which must lead to total mutual destruction, by a specific international agreement barring a nuclear armaments race.*

Prospects of Armaments Race

It could be suggested that the danger of destruction by nuclear weapons can be avoided—at least as far as this country is concerned—either by keeping our discoveries secret for an indefinite time, or else by developing our nucleonic armaments at such a pace that no other nations would think of attacking us from fear of overwhelming retaliation.

The answer to the first suggestion is that although we undoubtedly are at present ahead of the rest of the world in this field, the fundamental facts of nuclear power are a subject of common knowledge. . . . In other words, even if we can retain our leadership in basic knowledge of nucleonics for a certain time by maintaining secrecy as to all results achieved on this and associated Projects, it would be foolish to hope that this can protect us for more than a few years.

It may be asked whether we cannot prevent the development of military nucleonics in other countries by a monopoly on the raw materials of nuclear power. The answer is that even though the largest now known deposits of uranium ores are under the control of powers which belong to the "western" group . . . the old deposits in Czechoslovakia are outside this sphere. Russia is known to be mining radium on its own territory; and even if we do not know the size of the deposits discovered so far in the USSR, the probability that no large reserves of uranium will be found in a country which covers 1/5 of the land area of the earth . . . is too small to serve as a basis for security. *Thus, we cannot hope to avoid a nuclear armament race either by keeping secret from the competing nations the basic scientific facts of nuclear power or by cornering the raw materials required for such a race.*

We now . . . ask whether we could not feel ourselves safe in a race of nuclear armaments by virtue of our greater industrial potential, including greater diffusion of scientific and technical knowledge, greater volume and efficiency of our skilled labor corps, and greater experience of our management—all the factors whose importance has been so strikingly demonstrated in the conversion of this country into an arsenal of the Allied Nations in the present war. The answer is that all that these advantages can give us is the accumulation of a large number of bigger and better atomic bombs—and this only if we produce these bombs at the maximum of our capacity in peace time, and do not rely on conversion of a peace-time nucleonics industry to military production after the beginning of hostilities.

However, such a quantitative advantage in reserves of bottled destructive power will not make us safe from sudden attack. Just because a potential enemy will be afraid of being "outnumbered and outgunned," the temptation for him may be overwhelming to attempt a sudden unprovoked blow—particularly if he should suspect us of harboring aggressive intentions against his security or his sphere of influence. In no other type of warfare does the advantage lie so heavily with the aggressor. He can place his "infernal machines" in advance in all our major cities and explode them simultaneously, thus destroying a major part of our industry and a large part of our population, aggregated in densely populated metropolitan districts. . . .

Prospects of Agreement

[The] way in which the nuclear weapons now being secretly developed in this country are first revealed to the world appears to be of great, perhaps fateful importance.

One possible way—which may particularly appeal to those who consider nuclear bombs primarily as a secret weapon developed to help win the present war—is to use them without warning on an appropriately selected object in Japan. . . . Although important tactical results undoubtedly can be achieved by a sudden introduction of nuclear weapons, we nevertheless think that the question of the use of the very first available atomic bombs in the Japanese war should be weighed very carefully. . . . It may be very difficult to persuade the world that a nation which was capable of secretly preparing and suddenly releasing a weapon as indiscriminate as the rocket bomb and a million times more destructive, is to be trusted in its proclaimed desire of having such weapons abolished by international agreement. . . .

Thus, from the "optimistic" point of view—looking forward to an international agreement on the prevention of nuclear warfare—the military advantages and the saving of American lives achieved by the sudden use of atomic bombs against Japan may be outweighed by the ensuing loss of confidence and by a wave of horror and repulsion sweeping over the rest of the world and perhaps even dividing public opinion at home.

From this point of view, a demonstration of the new weapon might best be made, before the eyes of representatives of all the United Nations, on the desert or a barren island. The best possible atmosphere for the achievement of an international agreement could be achieved if America could say to the world, "You see what sort of a weapon we had but did not use. We are ready to renounce its use in the future if other nations join us in this renunciation and agree to the establishment of an efficient international control."

After such a demonstration the weapon might perhaps be used against Japan if the sanction of the United Nations (and of public opinion at home) were obtained, perhaps after a preliminary ultimatum to Japan to surrender or at least to evacuate certain regions as an alternative to their total destruction. . . .

Summary

To sum up, we urge that the use of nuclear bombs in this war be considered as a problem of long-range national policy rather than of military expediency, and that this policy be directed primarily to the achievement of an agreement permitting an effective international control of the means of nuclear warfare.

The vital importance of such a control for our country is obvious from the fact that the only effective alternative method of protecting this country appears to be a dispersal of our major cities and essential industries.

J. Gordon Arneson's Notes of Committee Meeting, May 31, 1945

(From Stoff, Fanton, and Williams, eds., *The Manhattan project: A Documentary Introduction to the Atomic Age.* New York: McGraw Hill, 1991, pp. 117–118.)

VIII. EFFECT OF THE BOMBING ON THE JAPANESE AND THEIR WILL TO FIGHT:

It was pointed out that one atomic bomb on an arsenal would not be much different from the effect caused by any Air Corps strike of present dimensions. However, <u>Dr. Oppenheimer</u> stated that the visual effect of an atomic bombing would be tremendous. It would be accompanied by a brilliant luminescence which would rise to a height of 10,000 to 20,000 feet. The neuron effect of the explosion would be dangerous to life for a radius of at least two-thirds of a mile.

After much discussion concerning various types of targets and the effects to be produced, <u>the Secretary expressed the conclusion, on which there was general agreement, that we could not give the Japanese any warning; that we could not concentrate in a civilian area; but that we should seek to make a profound psychological impression on as many of the inhabitants as possible. At the suggestion of Dr. Conant the Secretary agreed that the most desirable target would be a vital war plant employing a large number of workers and closely surrounded by workers' houses.</u>

There was some discussion of the desirability of attempting several strikes at the same time. <u>Dr. Oppenheimer's</u> judgement was that several strikes would be feasible. <u>General Groves,</u> however, expressed doubt about this proposal and pointed out the following objections: (1) We would lose the advantage of gaining additional knowledge concerning the weapon at each successive bombing; (2) such a program would require a rush job on the part of those assembling the bombs and might, therefore, be ineffective; (3) the effect would not be sufficiently distinct from our regular Air Force bombing program.

The Bombing Order

War Department
Office of the Chief of Staff

To: General Carl Spaatz
Commanding General
United States Army Strategic Air Forces

25 July 1945

1.   The 509 Composite Group, 20th Air Force will deliver its first special bomb as soon as weather will permit visual bombing after about 3 August 1945 on one of the targets: Hiroshima, Kokura, Niigata and Nagasaki. To carry military and civilian scientific personnel from

the War Department to observe and record the effects of the explosion of the bomb, additional aircraft will accompany the airplane carrying the bomb. The observing planes will stay several miles distant from the point of impact of the bomb.

2. Additional bombs will be delivered on the above targets as soon as made ready by the project staff. Further instructions will be issued concerning targets other than those listed above.

3. Dissemination of any and all information concerning the use of the weapon against Japan is reserved to the Secretary of War and President of the United States. No communiques on the subject or releases of information will be issued by Commanders in the field without specific prior authority. Any news stories will be sent to the War Department for special clearance.

4. The foregoing directive is issued to you by direction with the approval of the Secretary of War and of the Chief of Staff, USA. It is desired that you personally deliver one copy of this directive to General MacArthur and one copy to Admiral Nimitz for their information.

Thos J. Handy
General, G.S.C.
Acting Chief of Staff

Document E

Diary of President Harry S. Truman, July 1945

(As found in Robert Ferrell, ed., *Harry S. Truman and the Bomb: A Documentary History*. Worland, WY: High Plains Publishing, 1996, pp. 29–31.)

July 17

Just spent a couple of hours with Stalin. . . .

After the usual polite remarks we got down to business. I told Stalin that I am no diplomat but usually said yes and no to questions after hearing all the argument. It pleased him. I asked him if he had the agenda for the meeting. He said he had and that he had some more questions to present. I told him to fire away. He did and it is dynamite—but I have some dynamite too which I am not exploding now. He wants to fire Franco, to which I wouldn't object, and divide up the Italian colonies and other mandates, some no doubt that the British have. Then he got on the Chinese situation, told us what agreements had been reached and what was in abeyance. Most of the big points are settled. He'll be in the Jap war on August 15. Fini Japs when that comes about. . . .

July 18

. . . Went to lunch with P.M. at 1:30, walked around to British headquarters. Met at the gate by Mr. Churchill. . . . Discussed Manhattan (it is a success). Decided to tell Stalin about it. Stalin had told P.M. of telegram from Jap emperor asking for peace. Stalin also read his answer to me. It was satisfactory. Believe Japs will fold up before Russia comes in. I am sure they will when Manhattan appears over their homeland. I shall inform Stalin about it at an opportune time.

Stalin's luncheon was a most satisfactory meeting. I invited him to come to the U.S. . . . Said he was grossly misunderstood in U.S. and I was misunderstood in Russia. I told him that we each could help to remedy that situation in our home countries and that I intended to try with all I had to do my part at home. He gave me a most cordial smile and said he would do as much in Russia. . . .

July 25

We met at 11:00 a.m. today. That is, Stalin, Churchill, and the U.S. president. But I had a most important session with Lord Mountbatten and General Marshall before that. We have discovered the most terrible bomb in the history of the world. It may be the fire destruction prophesied in the Euphrates Valley era, after Noah and his fabulous ark. Anyway we think we have found the way to cause a disintegration of the atom. An experiment in the New Mexican desert was startling—to put it mildly. Thirteen pounds of the explosive caused the complete disintegration of a steel tower sixty feet high, created a crater six feet deep and twelve hundred feet in diameter, knocked over a steel tower a half mile away, and knocked men down ten thousand yards away. The explosion was visible for more than two hundred miles and audible for forty miles and more.

This weapon is to be used against Japan between now and August 10. I have told the secretary of war, Mr. Stimson, to use it so that military objectives and soldiers and sailors are the target and not women and children. . . . [We] cannot drop this terrible bomb on the old capital [Kyoto] or the new [Tokyo]. He and I are in accord. The target will be a purely military one and we will issue a warning statement asking the Japs to surrender and save lives. I'm sure they will not do that, but we will have given them the chance. It is certainly a good thing for the world that Hitler's crowd or Stalin's did not discover this atomic bomb. It seems to be the most terrible thing ever discovered, but it can be made the most useful.

Document F

Commentary of Soviet Foreign Minister Vyacheslav Molotov

(On the information presented by President Truman to Soviet leader Stalin on July 24,1945, at Potsdam.)

Truman decided to surprise us at Potsdam. . . . He took Stalin and me aside and—looking secretive—informed us that they had a secret weapon of an entirely new type, an extraordinary weapon. . . . It is hard to say what he was thinking, but it appeared to me that he wanted to dumbfound us. Stalin, however, reacted quite calmly and Truman decided that he didn't understand. The words "atomic bomb" hadn't been uttered, but we immediately guessed what was meant.

Document G

Extract from Memoirs of Marshal Zhukov

(In his memoirs, Soviet Marshal Zhukov recalled Stalin's reaction later on July 24, 1945.)

Stalin, in my presence, told Molotov about his conversation with Truman.
"They're raising the price," said Molotov.
Stalin gave a laugh, "Let them. We'll have a talk with [Igor] Kurchatov* today about speeding up our work."
I realized that they were talking about the creation of the atomic bomb.

Document H

Proclamation Defining Terms for the Japanese Surrender

(Signed at Potsdam and Issued by the President of the United States [Truman] and the Prime Minister of the United Kingdom [Attlee] and Concurred in by the President of the National Government of China [Chiang] , July 26, 1945.)

(1) We—the President of the United States, the President of the National Government of the Republic of China, and the Prime Minister of Great Britain, representing the hundreds of millions of our countrymen, have conferred and agree that Japan shall be given an opportunity to end this war.

(2) The prodigious land, sea and air forces of the United States, the British Empire and of China, many times reinforced by their armies and air fleets from the west, are poised to strike the final blows upon Japan. This military power is sustained and inspired by the determination of all the Allied Nations to prosecute the war against Japan until she ceases to resist.

(3) The result of the futile and senseless German resistance to the might of the aroused free peoples of the world stands forth in awful clarity as an example to the people to Japan. The might that now converges on Japan is immeasurably greater than that which, when applied to the resisting Nazis, necessarily laid waste to the lands, the industry and the method of life of the whole German people. The full application of our military power, backed by our resolve, will mean the inevitable and complete destruction of the Japanese armed forces and just as inevitably the utter devastation of the Japanese homeland.

(4) The time has come for Japan to decide whether she will continue to be controlled by those self-willed militaristic advisers whose unintelligent calculations have brought the Empire of Japan to the threshold of annihilation, or whether she will follow the path of reason.

(5) Following are our terms. We will not deviate from them. There are no alternatives. We shall brook no delay.

*The physicist who had been placed in charge of the Soviet nuclear project in 1943.

(6) There must be eliminated for all time the authority and influence of those who have deceived and misled the people of Japan into embarking on world conquest, for we insist that a new order of peace, security, and justice will be impossible until irresponsible militarism is driven from the world.

(7) Until such a new order is established *and* until there is convincing proof that Japan's war-making power is destroyed, points in Japanese territory to be designated by the Allies shall be occupied to secure the achievement of the basic objectives we are here setting forth.

(8) . . . Japanese sovereignty shall be limited to the islands of Honshu, Hokkaido, Kyushu, Shikoku and such minor islands as we determine.

(9) The Japanese military forces, after being completely disarmed, shall be permitted to return to their homes with the opportunity to lead peaceful and productive lives.

(10) We do not intend that the Japanese shall be enslaved as a race or destroyed as a nation, but stern justice shall be meted out to all war criminals, including those who have visited cruelties upon our prisoners. The Japanese Government shall remove all obstacles to the revival and strengthening of democratic tendencies among the Japanese people. Freedom of speech, of religion, and of thought, as well as respect for the fundamental human rights shall be established.

(11) Japan shall be permitted to maintain such industries as will sustain her economy and permit the exaction of just reparations in kind, but not those which would enable her to re-arm for war. To this end, access to, as distinguished from control of, raw materials shall be permitted. Eventual Japanese participation in world trade relations shall be permitted.

(12) The occupying forces of the Allies shall be withdrawn from Japan as soon as these objectives have been accomplished and there has been established in accordance with the freely expressed will of the Japanese people a peacefully inclined and responsible government.

(13) We call upon the government of Japan to proclaim now that unconditional surrender of all Japanese armed forces, and to provide proper and adequate assurances of their good faith in such action. The alternative for Japan is prompt and utter destruction.

Document I

Commentary of the Pacific War Research Society (Extract)

(As found in Pacific War Research Society, *The Day Man Lost Hiroshima, 6 August 1945.* Tokyo: Kodansha International Ltd., 1972.)

After her two daughters had left for the Deposit Bureau, Mrs. Hizume stood for a moment in the *genkan* to say goodbye to her husband, Tadayoshi. He was wearing the national wartime work uniform (called a *kokumin fuku*), with a field service cap on his head. Over his shoulder was slung a first aid kit. At ten minutes to eight he closed the front door behind him. Mrs. Hizume was now alone in the house.

She cleared away the breakfast things, then put some soy beans in a pot to soak in preparation for her family's evening meal. That finished, she went upstairs to hang out the laundry that she had done the previous evening. It was a hot clear day, with a slight breeze; the clothes, she thought as she stepped onto the wooden balcony, would not take long to dry.

The next thing she was aware of was a sudden blinding flash that seemed to sear her eyeballs; at the same time, her whole body felt as though a silvery current was flowing through it, and she heard a slight rushing sound, as of falling sand. Within a split second the current that she had felt passing through her body became a sensation of intense heat. Then she heard the crackle of burning hair. As she put her hands to her head, it seemed to her that every part of her was on fire. Without conscious thought, she ran inside and began to roll on the tatami, the straw mats that covered the floor, in an attempt to put out the flames that she felt were devouring her.

Then the whole house began to quiver. Rising from the floor, she now saw that countless bits of jagged glass had pierced her body; her arms and legs were bleeding; she could even feel the sharp fragments of glass in her face. Hardly knowing what she was doing, she crept downstairs, where the family kept the emergency first aid kit. The stairs too were strewn with broken glass. Then she saw that the walls of her house had caved in; the doors had been blown off; the house no longer had a roof. Outside, it was as dark as though the city had been enveloped in a heavy dust storm. What had happened?

At eight seconds past 8:16, the Little Boy had exploded. Fifty-one seconds previously it had been dropped from the bomb bay of the *Enola Gay* at a height of almost six miles. The three B-29s—the bomb carrier itself and the two observation planes—had turned sharply, as their pilots had been trained to do, and had fled the scene of imminent disaster. The explosion occurred at a height of 1,850 feet and less than 200 yards from the target point, the T-shaped Aioi Bridge that spanned the widest of the seven streams. The huge fireball that formed afterwards possessed, for a fraction of a second, a temperature of a million degrees. To many of the people who saw it, the fireball looked like a tremendous bluish white flash that blazed for about three seconds. The Little Boy had released the equivalent of 13,500 tons of TNT over the center of the city.

The point of explosion in the air is generally referred to as the epicenter; the point directly below it, on the ground, as the hypocenter. This latter was later determined to lie in the courtyard of Shima Hospital, in Saiku-machi. The intense heat of this man-made sun incinerated virtually everything within a radius of some five hundred yards of the hypocenter. Within a three-hundred-yard radius the heat waves traveled at a speed of around twelve hundred feet a second. Buildings as distant from the hypocenter as two miles or more were set ablaze. A thick cloud of smoke mushroomed into the sky to a height of forty thousand feet. The shock wave that followed immediately upon the explosion was felt well over a mile away from the hypocenter. Radioactivity within half a mile of the hypocenter was so intense that almost everyone who managed to survive both the heat and the blast was doomed to eventual death from the effects of radiation. Death, for some, was so sudden, so swift, they did not even have time to cry out in pain and shock; for others, who were badly burned or injured in other ways, death came more painfully, in a matter of minutes or hours or days; for still others, who were damaged internally by the radiation, death was a lingering affair. Some of the people who were in Hiroshima that morning are still, a quarter of a century later, suffering from the effects of "radiation sickness."

Statement by the President of the United States, August 6, 1945

Sixteen hours ago an American airplane dropped one bomb on [   ] and destroyed its usefulness to the enemy. That bomb had more power than 20,000 tons of T.N.T. It had more than two thousand times the blast power of the British "Grand Slam" which is the largest bomb ever yet used in the history of warfare.

The Japanese began the war from the air in Pearl Harbor. They have been repaid many fold. And the end is not yet. With this bomb we have now added a new and revolutionary increase in destruction to supplement the growing power of our armed forces. In their present form these bombs are now in production and even more powerful forms are in development.

It is an atomic bomb. It is a harnessing of the basic power of the universe. The force from which the sun draws its power has been loosed against those who brought war to the Far East.

Before 1939, it was the accepted belief of scientists that it was theoretically possible to release atomic energy. But no one knew any practical method of doing it. By 1942, however, we knew that the Germans were working feverishly to find a way to add atomic energy to the other engines of war with which they hoped to enslave the world. But they failed. We may be grateful to Providence that the Germans got the V-1's and V-2's late and in limited quantities and even more grateful that they did not get the atomic bomb at all.

The battle of the laboratories held fateful risks for us as well as the battles of the air, land and sea, and we have now won the battle of the laboratories as we have won the other battles. . . .

We have spent two billion dollars on the greatest scientific gamble in history—and won. . . .

We are now prepared to obliterate more rapidly and completely every productive enterprise the Japanese have above ground in any city. We shall destroy their docks, their factories, and their communications. Let there be no mistake; we shall completely destroy Japan's power to make war.

It was to spare the Japanese people from utter destruction that the ultimatum of July 26 was issued at Potsdam. Their leaders promptly rejected that ultimatum. If they do not now accept our terms they may expect a rain of ruin from the air, the like of which has never been seen on this earth. Behind this air attack will follow sea and land forces in such numbers and power as they have not yet seen and with the fighting skill of which they are already well aware. . . .

It has never been the habit of the scientists of this country or the policy of this Government to withhold from the world scientific knowledge. Normally, therefore, everything about the work with atomic energy would be made public.

But under present circumstances it is not intended to divulge the technical processes of production or all the military applications, pending further examination of possible methods of protecting us and the rest of the world from the danger of sudden destruction.

I shall recommend that the Congress of the United States consider promptly the establishment of an appropriate commission to control the production and use of atomic power within the United States. I shall give further consideration and make further recommendations to the Congress as to how atomic power can become a powerful and forceful influence towards the maintenance of world peace.

Truman's Memoirs (Extract)

(From *Memoirs by Harry S. Truman: Vol. 1: Year of Decisions*. New York: Doubleday and Company, 1955, pp. 415–419.)

The historic message of the first explosion of an atomic bomb was flashed to me in a message from Secretary of War Stimson on the morning of July 16. . . . We were now in possession of a weapon that would not only revolutionize war but could alter the course of history and civilization. . . . On July 24 I casually mentioned to Stalin that we had a new weapon of unusual destructive force. The Russian Premier showed no special interest. All he said was that he was glad to hear and hoped we would make "good use of it against the Japanese.". . . If the test of the bomb was successful, I wanted to afford Japan a clear chance to end the fighting before we made use of this newly gained power. . . . General Marshall told me it might cost half a million American lives to force the enemy's surrender on his home grounds.

But now the test was successful. The entire development of the atomic bomb had been dictated by military considerations. . . . It was their recommendation [the advisory committee] that the bomb be used against the enemy as soon as it could be done. They recommended further that it should be used without specific warning and against a target that would clearly show its devastating strength. I had realized, of course, that an atomic bomb explosion would inflict damage and casualties beyond imagination. On the other hand, the scientific advisors of the committee reported, "we can propose no technical demonstration likely to bring an end to the war; we can see no alternative to direct military use.". . . The final decision of where and when to use the atomic bomb was up to me. Let there be no mistake about it. I regarded the bomb as a military weapon and never had any doubt that it should be used.

Resources

Bibliography

Allen, Thomas B., and Norman Polmar. *Code-Name Downfall: The Secret Plan to Invade Japan and Why Truman Dropped the Bomb*. New York: Simon & Schuster, 1995.

Alperovitz, Gar. *The Decision to Use the Atomic Bomb and the Architecture of an American Myth*. New York: Knopf, 1995.

Bird, Kai, and Lawrence Lifschultz, eds. *Hiroshima's Shadow: Writings on the Denial of History and Smithsonian Controversy*. Stony Creek, CT: The Pamphleters Press, 1998.

The Committee for the Compilation of Materials on Damage Caused by the Atomic Bombs in Hiroshima and Nagasaki. *Hiroshima and Nagasaki: The Physical, Medical, and Social Effects of the Atomic Bombings*, trans. Eisei Ishikawa and David L. Swain. New York: Basic Books, 1981.

Feifer, George. *Tenozan: The Battle of Okinawa and the Atomic Bomb*. New York: Ticknor & Fields, 1992.

Feis, Herbert. *The Atomic Bomb and the End of World War II*. Princeton: Princeton University Press, 1970.

Ferrell, Robert, ed. *Harry S. Truman and the Bomb: a Documentary History*. Worland, WY: High Plains Publishing, 1996.

Goldstein, Donald M., Katherine V. Dillon, and J. Michael Wenger. *Rain of Ruin: A Photographic History of Hiroshima and Nagasaki*. Washington, DC: Brassey's, 1995.

Holloway, David. *Stalin and the Bomb: The Soviet Union and Atomic Energy, 1939–1956*. New Haven: Yale University Press, 1994.

Leffler, Melvyn P. *A Preponderance of Power: National Security, the Truman Administration and the Cold War*. Stanford, CA: Stanford University Press, 1992.

Markowitz, Norman D. *The Rise and Fall of The People's Century: Henry A. Wallace and American Liberalism, 1941–1948*. New York: Free Press, 1973.

McCullough, David. *Truman*. New York: Simon and Schuster, 1992.

Moskin, Robert. *Mr. Truman's War: The Final Victories of World War II and the Birth of the Postwar World*. New York: Random House, 1996.

Pacific War Research Society. *The Day Man Lost Hiroshima, 6 August 1945*. Tokyo: Kodansha International Ltd., 1972.

Thomas, Gordon, and Max Morgan Witts. *Ruin from the Air: The Enola Gay's Atomic Mission to Hiroshima*. New York: Steinday, 1977.

Truman, Harry. *Autobiography of Harry S. Truman*, ed. Robert Ferrell. Boulder: Colorado University Press, 1980.

Wainstock, Dennis. *The Decision to Drop the Atomic Bomb*. Westport, CT: Praeger, 1996.

Weyden, Peter. *Day One: Before Hiroshima and After*. New York: Simon & Schuster, 1984.

Wilcox, Robert K. *Japan's Secret War: Japan's Race Against Time to Build Its Own Atomic Bomb*. New York: Marlowe & Co., 1995.

Media Resources

Documentaries

The Decision to Drop the Bomb. 85 min. 1965. A day-by-day accounting of the last months before the bombs were dropped. Herbert Feis (the leading "official" historian of the bomb's use) and Gar Alperovitz (the leading "revisionist" historian on the subject) acted as advisors on the film.

Enola Gay *and the Atomic Bombing of Japan*. 75 minutes. A History Channel documentary. Available from Teacher's Video, 800-262-8837.

Hiroshima and Nagasaki: Was Truman's Decision to Use the Bomb Justified? 20 minutes. A book, *President Truman and the Atomic Bomb*, and a CD-ROM for either Macintosh or Windows entitled *Critical Mass: America's Race to Build the Atomic Bomb* (1996) are available from the same source. Available from Zenger Media, 800-421-4246.

Hiroshima: Hallmark/Showtime Presents. 165 minutes. 1995. Available from Zenger Media, 800-421-4246.

Hiroshima: The Decision to Drop the Bomb. 75 minutes. 1995. An Arts and Entertainment (A&E) documentary. Available from Teacher's Video, 800-262-8837.

Hiroshima—Why the Bomb Was Dropped: A Peter Jennings/ABC News Report. 70 minutes. 1995. Available from Zenger Media, 800-421-4246.

J. Robert Oppenheimer. 50 minutes. A program in the Arts and Entertainment (A&E) series *Biography*. Available from Teacher's Video, 800-421-8837.

Truman. 240 minutes. 1997. A four-part program from the PBS series *The American Experience*. Part 2, "The Moon, Stars, and All the Planets," is especially good. Available on two videocassettes from PBS Video, 800-344-3337.

Truman and the Atomic Bomb. 15 minutes. St. Cloud: Central Minnesota Educational Research and Development Council, 1969.

Feature Films

Above and Beyond. 122 min. MGM Home Entertainment, 1953. Focuses on the 509th Composite Group: its commander, Army-Air Force Colonel Paul Tibbets; the pilot of the *Enola Gay*; and its mission to Hiroshima. Available from Movies Unlimited, 800-4 MOVIES.

Day One. 141 minutes. 1989. A television film of Peter Weyden's book, it dramatizes the race to build the atomic bomb. Available from Worldvision Home Video, 212-261-2700.

Fat Man and Little Boy. 127 minutes. Paramount Home Video, 1989. Stars Paul Newman as General Leslie Groves in a more fictionalized version of the Manhattan Project story. John Cusack plays a fictional, idealized scientist who raises some interesting issues. Available from Movies Unlimited, 800-4 MOVIES.

Give Em Hell, Harry! 103 minutes. 1975. The film version of James Whitmore's one-man stage performance using Truman's words. Available from Wordvision Home Video, 212-261-2700.

Truman. 135 minutes. HBO Home Video, 1995. A cable television docudrama based on David McCullough's biography, it stars Gary Sinise as the president. Available from Facets Multimedia, 800-331-6197.

Educational Media

"The Day After Trinity" is a CD-ROM enhanced version of Jon Else's award-winning film on J. Robert Oppenheimer and the atomic bomb. It can be played on either a MAC or Windows platform. Available from Voyager, 212-219-2522.

"Critical Mass: Americas's Race to Build the Atomic Bomb" is a CD-ROM for Windows that explores the technology, politics, and consequences of the bomb project. It is available from Corbis, 206-641-4505.

UNIT 12

César Chávez and Migrant Farm Workers

HISTORICAL BACKGROUND

César Chávez was born in Arizona in 1927, into an immigrant Mexican farm family. Although his family owned their farm, the Depression, combined with a severe drought, wiped them out in 1937. The Chávez family became migrant farm workers, moving from job to job in California. During that period, California agricultural and cannery workers began the first, unsuccessful attempts to organize themselves. While he was in school, Chávez worked in the fields to help support his family. At work and at school, Chávez felt that people of Mexican descent were discriminated against in California. Chávez began to complain about working conditions, but was unable to do anything on his own. In 1944 Chávez joined the Navy and served until the end of the war.

When he came home, Chávez went back to work in the fields. In 1948 he married Helen Fabela, and together they worked to educate Mexican immigrants and to help them gain citizenship. Soon afterwards, he joined the Community Service Organization and began to work for immigrant rights full time. In 1962 he quit in order to devote himself to unionizing the field workers. This led to a confrontation in Delano, California, in 1965, as the grape pickers went on strike and the growers brought in replacements. Chávez was arrested repeatedly during the strike, but finally won some concessions in 1970.

The same year, Chávez led a strike against lettuce growers. It was a long struggle, finally resolved in 1978 with a wage increase for workers to $3.53 per hour from the $1.20 per hour in effect since 1965. At the height of Chávez's efforts, the United Farm Workers grew to some 80,000 members. Until his death in 1993, Chávez continued to work for *La Causa*—to improve the rights and working conditions of migrant farm workers. His death, increased national upset over illegal immigration, especially across the Mexican-U.S. border, and renewed pressure from California agribusiness for cheap labor on the "bracero" model*—all have left the United Farm Workers struggling to rebuild membership and bargaining power.

* The word *bracero* comes from the Spanish word *brazas*, arms. The "bracero" program was created by the U.S. government in 1942 to recruit contracted "guest" workers from Mexico to help the war effort in agriculture. They harvested crops in 21 states and were to return to Mexico when their contracts ended. Although their living and working conditions were protected by regulations, these were almost never enforced.

Key Questions About This Subject

- Under what circumstances is civil disobedience justified by "higher" moral, social, or political concerns?
- How impartial are local ordinances in regions where the powerless are struggling against entrenched interests?
- What should be the limits of governmental jurisdiction over labor and workplace conditions, in terms both of covered industries and legal status of the workers?
- What forms of protection and redress exist for migrant laborers?
- How far beyond the organization of the workers themselves should a union go to pressure businesses to accede to its demands?
- What role should government play in these kinds of disputes?*

Mock Trial

If you are going to hold a simulated trial, here are the charges against César Chávez (the Defendant): César Chávez, a union organizer, is accused of disturbing the peace and inciting to riot as he attempted to organize migrant farm laborers.

* It was alleged that the Department of Defense was ordered to increase its purchases of grapes and raisins to offset the effectiveness of the UFW grape boycott.

DOCUMENTS

Document A

Statement from the United Farm Workers

(by César Chávez, "God is Beside You on the Picket Line," March, 1966.)

In the [250 mile] "March from Delano [California] to Sacramento [the state capital]" there is a meeting of cultures and traditions; the centuries-old religous tradition of Spanish culture conjoins with the very contemporary cultural syndrome of "demonstration" springing from the spontaneity of the poor, the downtrodden, the rejected, the discriminated against bearing visibly their need and demand for equality and freedom.

In every religion-oriented culture "the pilgrimage" has had a place: a trip made with sacrifice and hardship as an expression of penance and of commitment—and often involving a petition to the patron of the pilgrimage for some sincerely sought benefit of body or soul. Pilgrimage has not passed from Mexican culture. . . .

But throughout the Spanish-speaking world there is another tradition that touched the present march, that of the Lenten penitential processions. . . .The penitential procession is

Critical Thinking Using Primary Sources in U.S. History

also in the blood of the Mexican-American, and the Delano march will therefore be one of penance—public penance for the sins of the strikers, their own personal sins as well as their yielding perhaps to feelings of hatred and revenge in the strike itself. They hope by the march to set themselves at peace with the Lord, so that the justice of their cause will be purified of all lesser motivation.

These two great traditions of a great people meet in the Mexican-American with the belief that Delano [is] his "cause," his great demand for justice, freedom, and respect from a predominantly foreign cultural community in a land where he was first. The revolutions of Mexico were primarily uprisings of the poor, fighting for bread and for dignity. The Mexican-American is also a child of the revolution.

Pilgrimage, penance, and revolution. The pilgrimage from Delano to Sacramento has strong religio-cultural overtones. But it is also the pilgrimage of a cultural minority which has suffered from a hostile environment, and a minority which means business.

Document B

Appeal of César Chávez's Conviction

(Court of Appeals of California, Fifth Appellate District, November 20, 1967; appeal of the decision by a Municipal Court in Tulare County.)

A criminal complaint was filed in the Justice Court of the Porterville Judicial District charging appellant [César Chávez] with the illegal use of a speaker mounted on a vehicle in violation of Tulare County's Loud Speaker Control Ordinance. Appellant demurred to the complaint and when the court overruled his demurrer he petitioned the Superior Court of Tulare County for a writ of prohibition. Appellant's petition was denied and this appeal followed. . . .

We have carefully reviewed the Tulare County ordinance with these salutary principles in mind and conclude that the ordinance is unconstitutional. . . .

The Tulare ordinance presents great opportunity for discrimination, political preference and the type of censorship that is repugnant to the very concept upon which our free form of government is founded. . . .

[T]he ordinance makes it possible for the board to purposely engage in delaying tactics which could be extremely detrimental, if not fatal, to the presentation of vital issues in labor disputes, political campaigns and similar national, state or local matters which are by nature transitory. . . .

Commentary of César Chávez

(From Jacques Levy, *César Chávez: Autobiography of La Causa*. New York: Norton, 1975, pp. 201–203.)

One of our most powerful nonviolent weapons is the economic boycott. Alone, the farm workers have no economic power; but with the help of the public they can develop the economic power to counter that of the growers.

We started the grape boycott helter skelter in October 1965, about a month after the strike started. We had to organize the people first, so they could be more effective and more disciplined. Then, in November, we started putting picket lines wherever the grapes went. We began to send the people to San Francisco and Los Angeles and to have them follow the truckloads of grapes.

When we set up a picket line at one of the piers in San Francisco, all the longshoremen walked out. They, of course, wouldn't go to work unless we left. So we got the ILWU (International Longshoremen's and Warehousemen's Union) in trouble, but they wouldn't tell us to leave.

I especially remember, though, a call from Al Green of AWOC trying to convince me to take the picket line off. I couldn't see any reason why I should, just because it was embarrassing him with the other unions. . . .

He was so angry, he cussed me, and I cussed him back. In fact, I not only cussed him back, I went at him on the phone, really tore him up. I was so mad, he finally realized it and pulled back. . . .

We stopped scab grapes from being loaded on the S.S. *President Wilson* which was bound for Asia. Later, longshoremen refused to load scab grapes on the *Burrard*, the *Rio Negro*, and other ships.

As time went on, we began to form a strategy. Experience told us what to do. We decided to concentrate the boycott on Schenley and sent out volunteers to major cities across the country. The Schenley wine boycott started in full earnest the middle of December.

Speech by César E. Chávez, January 12, 1990

My friends, today we honor a giant among men: today we honor the [R]everend Martin Luther King, Jr. . . .

Today we honor a wise teacher, an inspiring leader, and a true visionary, but to truly honor Dr. King we must do more than say words of praise.

We must learn his lessons and put his views into practice, so that we may truly be free at last. . . .

Dr. King knew that he very probably wouldn't survive the struggle that he led so well. But he said "If I am stopped, the movement will not stop. If I am stopped, our work will not stop. For what we are doing is right. What we're doing is just, and [G]od is with us."

My friends, as we enter a new decade, it should be clear to all of us that there is an unfinished agenda, that we have miles to go before we reach the promised land.

The men who rule this country today never learned the lessons of Dr. King, they never learned that non-violence is the only way to peace and justice.

Our nation continues to wage war upon its neighbors, and upon itself.

The powers that be rule over a racist society, filled with hatred and ignorance.

Our nation continues to be segregated along racial and economical lines.

The powers that be make themselves richer by exploiting the poor. Our nation continues to allow children to go hungry, and will not even house its own people. . . .

The United Farm Workers are dedicated to carrying on the dream of [R]everend Martin Luther King, Jr. My friends, I would like to tell you about the struggle of the Farm workers who are waging a desperate struggle for our rights, for our children's rights and for our very lives.

Many decades ago the chemical industry promised the growers that pesticides would bring great wealth and bountiful harvests to the fields.

Just recently, the experts are learning what farm workers, and the truly organized farmers have known for years.

The prestigious National Academy of Sciences recently concluded an exhaustive five-year study which determined that pesticides do not improve profits and do not produce more crops.

What, then, is the effect of pesticides? Pesticides have created a legacy of pain, and misery, and death for farm workers and consumers alike.

The crop which poses the greatest danger, and the focus of our struggle, is the table grape crop. These pesticides soak the fields. Drift with the wind, pollute the water, and are eaten by unwitting consumers. . . .

And the children are dying.

They are dying slow, painful, cruel deaths in towns called cancer clusters, in cancer clusters like McFarland, where the children cancer rate is 800 percent above normal. . . .

My friends, the suffering must end. So many children are dying, so many babies are born without limbs and vital organs, so many workers are dying in the fields.

We have no choice, we must stop the plague of pesticides.

The growers responsible for this outrage are blinded by greed, by racism, and by power.

The same inhumanity displayed at Selma, in Birmingham, in so many of Dr. King's battle-grounds, is displayed every day in the vineyards of California.

The farm labor system in place today is a system of economic slavery. . . .

Our workers labor for many hours every day under the hot sun, often without safe drinking water or toilet facilities.

Our workers are constantly subjected to incredible pressures and intimidation to meet excessive quotas.

The women who work in the fields are routinely subjected to sexual harassment and sexual assaults by the grower's thugs. When our workers complain, or try to organize, they are fired, assaulted, and even murdered. . . .

We are winning, but there is still much hard work ahead of us. I hope that you will join our struggle. The simple act of refusing to buy table grapes laced with pesticides is a powerful statement that the growers understand.

Economic pressure is the only language the growers speak, and they are beginning to listen.

Please, boycott table grapes. For your safety, for the workers, and for the children, we must act together.

My friends, Dr. King realized that the only real wealth comes from helping others. . . .

Chávez Quotations

(From "Education of the Heart: César E. Chávez in His Own Words." César E. Chávez Foundation, 1995.)

Being of service is not enough. You must become a servant of the people. When you do, you can demand their commitment in return.

In this world it is possible to achieve great material wealth, to live an opulent life. But a life built upon those things alone leaves a shallow legacy, in the end, we will be judged by other standards.

We cannot seek achievement for ourselves and forget about progress and prosperity for our community. . . . Our ambitions must be broad enough to include the aspirations and needs of others, for their sakes and for our own.

We need to help students and parents cherish and preserve the ethnic and cultural diversity that nourishes and strengthens this community and this nation.

Do not romanticize the poor. . . . We are all people, human beings subject to the same temptations and faults as all others. Our poverty damages our dignity.

What is at stake is human dignity. If a man is not accorded respect he cannot respect himself and if he does not respect himself, he cannot demand it.

Real education should consist of drawing the goodness and the best out of our own students. What better books can there be than the book of humanity?

The end of all education should surely be service to others.

It is not enough to teach our young people to be successful . . . so they can realize their ambitions, so they can earn good livings, so they can accumulate the material things that this society bestows. Those are worthwhile goals. But it is not enough to progress as individuals while our friends and neighbors are left behind.

People who have lost their hunger for justice are not ultimately powerful. They are like sick people who have lost their appetite for what is truly nourishing. Such sick people should not frighten or discourage us. They should be prayed for along with the sick people who are in the hospital.

Violence just hurts those who are already hurt. . . . Instead of exposing the brutality of the oppressor, it justifies it.

We are convinced that non-violence is more powerful than violence. We are convinced that non-violence supports you if you have a just moral cause. . . . If you use violence, you have to sell part of yourself for that violence. Then you are no longer a master of your own struggle.

It's amazing how people can get so excited about a rocket to the moon and not give a damn about smog, oil leaks, the devastation of the environment with pesticides, hunger, disease. When the poor share some of the power that the affluent now monopolize, we will give a damn.

Because we have suffered, and we are not afraid to suffer in order to survive, we are ready to give up everything—even our lives—in our struggle for justice.

Resources

Bibliography

Altman, Linda Jacobs. *César Chávez*. San Diego: Lucent Books, 1996.

Cedeno, Maria E. *César Chávez, Labor Leader*. Brookfield, CT: Millbrook Press, 1994.

Collins, David R. *Farmworker's Friend: The Story of César Chávez*. Minneapolis: Lerner Publishing Group, 1996.

Daniel, Cletus E. *Bitter Harvest: A History of California, 1870–1941*. Ithaca, NY: Cornell University Press, 1981.

Davis, Lucile. *César Chávez: A Photo-Illustrated Biography*. Mankato, MN: Capstone Press, 1997.

Day, Mark. *Forty Acres: César Chávez and the Farmworkers*. New York: Praeger, 1971.

Del Castillo, Richard Griswold, and Richard A. Garcia. *César Chávez: A Triumph of Spirit*. Norman: University of Oklahoma Press, 1997.

Dunne, John D. *Delano*. New York: Farrar, Straus & Giroux, 1971.

Ferriss, Susan, Ricardo Sandoval, and Diana Hembree, eds. *The Fight in the Fields: César Chávez and the Farmworkers Movement*. New York: Harcourt Brace, 1998.

Gonzales, Doreen. *César Chávez: Leader for Migrant Farm Workers*. Springfield, NJ: Enslow Publishers, 1996.

Jelinik, Laurence J. *Harvest Empire: A History of California Agriculture*, 2nd ed. San Francisco: Boyd and Fraser, 1982.

Levy, Jacques. *César Chávez: An Autobiography of La Causa*. New York: Norton, 1975.

Ross, Fred. *Conquering Goliath: César Chávez at the Beginning*. Detroit: Wayne State University Press, 1992.

Rothenberg, Daniel. *With These Hands: The Hidden World of Migrant Farmworkers Today*. New York: Harcourt Brace, 1998.

Shindo, Charles J. *Dust Bowl Migrants in the American Imagination*. Lawrence: University Press of Kansas, 1997.

Strazzabosco, Jeanne M. *Learning About Justice from the Life of César Chávez*. New York: Rosen Publishing Group, 1997.

Taylor, Ronald B. *Chávez and the Farm Workers*. Boston: Beacon Press, 1975.

Media Resources

Documentaries

Chicano! History of the Mexican American Civil Rights Movement. 228 minutes. 1996. Four-part video series with an index, posters, and guide. Part 2 covers *The Struggle in the Fields* (57 minutes). A companion book and a CD-ROM in Spanish and English, *Chicano!*, are also available. Available from Social Studies School Service, 800-421-4246.

Common Man, Uncommon Vision: The César Chávez Story. 48 minutes. Z65 Communications, 1995. Narrated by Martin Sheen, it comes with a study guide.

The Fight in the Fields: César Chávez and the Farm Workers' Struggle. 1996. Available from PBS Video, 800-344-3337.

Harvest of Shame. 53 minutes. CRM/McGraw-Hill Films, 1960. Black-and-white documentary from the series *CBS Reports*. Available from Zenger Media, 800-421-4246.

Strawberries: The Fruit of Injustice. 8 minutes. United Farm Workers of America, 1996. Directed by Yu Li and narrated by Martin Sheen. Available from the UFW store at www.ufw.org.

Feature Films

The Grapes of Wrath. 129 minutes. 1940. John Ford's adaptation of John Steinbeck's 1939 novel about an earlier generation of migrant farmers. Available from Teacher's Video Company, 800-262-8837.

The Milagro Beanfield War. 118 minutes. 1988. Based on John Nichols' novel about New Mexican farmers and townspeople opposing development. Available at many local video stores.

My Family/Mi Familia. 126 minutes. 1994. A multi-generational saga about the Sanchez family in Los Angeles, it covers more than 60 years, from early in 1900 when the family patriarch came north from Mexico. Available at many local video stores.

Of Mice and Men. 110 minutes. 1992. Film adaptation of John Steinbeck's novel. Available from Teacher's Video Company, 800-262-8837.

Salt of the Earth. 94 minutes. 1951. Film made by blacklisted Hollywood writers and directors about an unsuccessful Mexican-American miners' strike in New Mexico. Available from Zenger Media, 800-421-4246.

UNIT 13

Gloria Steinem and the Women's Movement

HISTORICAL BACKGROUND

Gloria Steinem was born in 1934 in Toledo, Ohio. Her father was an itinerant businessman who dabbled in various schemes but never had a permanent office or job. Her mother was well educated and had worked as a journalist before giving up her career when she married. Steinem's mother was clinically depressed and had many breakdowns. The Steinems divorced in the mid-1940s, and Gloria became her mother's caretaker. Although the Steinems had been middle class, Gloria lived at near poverty level while caring for her mother in a small basement apartment barely large enough for two people.

A turning point came in Steinem's life when her older sister took over the responsibility for their mother. Together, they lived in Washington, D.C., where Steinem graduated from high school. In 1952 she entered Smith College for women in Northampton, Massachusetts. Money was a big issue all the way through college, but Steinem was able to scrape by with scholarships and odd jobs. Steinem spent her junior year abroad in Geneva, Switzerland and a summer studying at Oxford. She graduated in 1956 magna cum laude with a major in government.

After graduation Steinem spent nearly two years in India on a Chester Bowles Asian Fellowship. She tried to avoid the westernized cities of India and spent most of her time with the common people, traveling in third-class railroad cars and living in small villages. Steinem worked with followers of Gandhi and became very influenced by his works and philosophy.

In 1960 Steinem moved to New York City to work as a writer. She first received national recognition for a magazine article titled "I Was a Playboy Bunny." Steinem had worked undercover as a "Bunny" at a Playboy Club to gather information for her writing and was appalled at the sexist treatment women received. She began to write for national publications, becoming a noted feminist with the publication of an essay in 1964 called "After Black Power, Women's Liberation."

Throughout the '60s, Steinem was active in the antiwar movement, the McGovern campaign for president, and the abortion rights movement. She also supported César Chávez and *La Causa*, his movement on behalf of farm workers.

In 1970 Steinem helped to found the Women's Action Alliance. In 1971, she helped found the National Women's Political Caucus, which encouraged women to run for political office. In January 1972, Steinem and others founded *Ms.* magazine, which became the feminist movement's national forum. Throughout the '70s and '80s Steinem continued to be a political activist, particularly on issues dealing with women—fair employment and wages, daycare, abortion, and political and economic empowerment.

Although not as much in the spotlight recently, Steinem has continued to write. *Outrageous Acts and Everyday Rebellions* (1983) contains some of her more important writings. She also wrote a biography of Marilyn Monroe and *Moving Beyond Words* (1994), a collection of essays.

Critical Thinking Using Primary Sources in U.S. History

Key Questions About This Subject

- What events in the twentieth century were turning points for women who wanted to work outside the home?
- What is the "glass ceiling," and how have women been able to break through it?
- Why were some people, like Phyllis Schlafly and Jerry Falwell, against women taking jobs outside the home?

- According to advocates like Gloria Steinem, why is money not as important as the ability of a woman to have a career?
- What major breakthroughs in the women's movement have occurred in the last 20 years economically, socially, and politically?

Mock Trial

If you are going to hold a simulated trial, here are the charges against Gloria Steinem (the Defendant): Gloria Steinem, professional writer, is charged with fomenting discontent and disturbing the peace by encouraging the breakup of traditional family structure and gender roles.

DOCUMENTS

Document A

Address at the 1954 Smith College Graduation, Given by Alistair Cooke

(From the *Smith Alumnae Bulletin*, August 1954. As found in Carolyn G. Heilbrun, *The Education of a Woman: The Life of Gloria Steinem*. New York: Dial Press, 1995, pp. 60–61.

At this moment [he assured the young women], ridiculous though it may seem, the fortune of you here is being decided by anonymous young men who are packing their bags in New Haven, Connecticut, in Cambridge, Massachusetts, Princeton, New Jersey, Williamstown, even perhaps in Grinnell, Iowa. . . . It may not be the proper thing for a commencement speaker to begin this way by wishing you a happy marriage. But. . . . since it is the supreme role which all of you will sooner or later hanker after, even the art students and sociologists among you, it seems to me realistic to start by recognizing, on this spring morning, the main direction in which your fancies turn.

Excerpts from "The Problem That Has No Name"

(From Betty Friedan, *The Feminine Mystique*. New York: W.W. Nortorn, 1963, pp. 11–16, 21–22, and 27. As found in Mary Beth Norton and Ruth M. Alexander, eds., *Major Problems in American Women's History*, 2nd ed. Lexington, MA: D.C. Heath and Co., 1996, pp. 439–442.)

The problem lay buried, unspoken, for many years in the minds of American women. It was a strange stirring, a sense of dissatisfaction, a yearning that women suffered in the middle of the twentieth century in the United States. Each suburban wife struggled with it alone. As she made the beds, shopped for groceries, matched slipcover material, ate peanut butter sandwiches with her children, chauffeured Cub Scouts and Brownies, lay beside her husband at night—she was afraid to ask even of herself the silent question—"Is this all?"

The suburban housewife—she was the dream image of the young American woman and the envy, it was said, of women all over the world. The American housewife—freed by science and labor-saving appliances from the drudgery, the dangers of childbirth and the illnesses of her grandmother. She was healthy, beautiful, educated, concerned only about her husband, her children, her home. She had found true feminine fulfillment. . . .

In the fifteen years after World War II, this mystique of feminine fulfillment became the cherished and self-perpetuating core of contemporary American culture. Millions of women lived their lives in the image of those pretty pictures of the American suburban housewife, kissing their husbands goodbye in front of the picture window, depositing their stationwagonsful of children at school, and smiling as they ran the new electric waxer over the spotless kitchen floor. They baked their own bread, sewed their own and their children's clothes, kept their new washing machines and dryers running all day. They changed the sheets on the beds twice a week instead of once, took the rug-hooking class in adult education, and pitied their poor frustrated mothers, who had dreamed of having a career. Their only dream was to be perfect wives and mothers; their highest ambition to have five children and a beautiful house, their only fight to get and keep their husbands. . . .

If a woman had a problem in the 1950's and 1960's, she knew that something must be wrong with her marriage, or with herself. Other women were satisfied with their lives, she thought. What kind of woman was she if she did not feel this mysterious fulfillment waxing the kitchen floor? She was so ashamed to admit her dissatisfaction that she never knew how many other women shared it. If she tried to tell her husband, he didn't understand what she was talking about. . . .

If I am right, the problem that has no name stirring in the minds of so many American women today is not a matter of loss of femininity or too much education, or the demands of domesticity. It is far more important than anyone recognizes. It is the key to these other new and old problems which have been torturing women and their husbands and children, and puzzling their doctors and educators for years. It may well be the key to our future as a nation and a culture. We can no longer ignore that voice within women that says: "I want something more than my husband and my children and my home."

Document C

Jerry Falwell's Views on the ERA, 1980

(Excerpt from Jerry Falwell, *Listen America*. New York: Doubleday, 1980, pp. 150–151. As found in Mary Beth Norton and Ruth M. Alexander, eds., *Major Problems in American Women's History,* 2nd ed. Lexington, MA: D.C. Heath and Co., 1996, pp. 491–492.)

I believe that at the foundation of the women's liberation movement there is a minority core of women who were once bored with life, whose real problems are spiritual problems. Many women have never accepted their God-given roles. They live in disobedience to God's laws and have promoted their godless philosophy throughout our society. God Almighty created men and women biologically different and with differing needs and roles. He made men and women to complement each other and to love each other. Not all women involved in the feminist movement are radicals. Some are misinformed, and some are lonely women who like being housewives and helpmeets and mothers, but whose husbands spend little time at home and who take no interest in their wives and children. Sometimes the full load of rearing a family becomes a great burden to a woman who is not supported by a man. Women who work should be respected and accorded dignity and equal rewards for equal work. But this is not what the present feminist movement and equal rights movement are all about. . . .

The Equal Rights Amendment strikes at the foundation of our entire social structure. If passed, this amendment would accomplish exactly the opposite of its outward claims. By mandating absolute equality under the law, it will actually take away many of the special rights women now enjoy. ERA is not merely a political issue, but a moral issue as well. A definite violation of holy Scripture, ERA defies the mandate that "the husband is the head of the wife, even as Christ is the head of the church" (Ep. 5:23). In 1 Peter 3:7 we read that husbands are to give their wives honor as unto the weaker vessel, that they are both heirs together of the grace of life. Because a woman is weaker does not mean that she is less important.

Document D

Excerpts from *The Power of the Positive Woman*

(From Phyllis Schlafly, *The Power of the Positive Woman*. New Rochelle, NY: Arlington House Publishers, 1977, pp. 45–50.)

Marriage and motherhood have always been the number-one career choice of the large majority of women. Are they still a viable career choice for the modern woman? . . . Are they, as the women's liberation movement would have us believe, an anachronism from a bygone era, the institutionalized serfdom (or "legalized prostitution") from which women must be freed if they are to find their own identity and self-fulfillment?

What is it that the women's liberation movement invites women to be liberated from? An objective reading of the liberation movement literature compels the conclusion that the answer must be marriage, home, husband, family, and children—because, by definition, those are all evidences of the "second-class status" of women. . . .

What does a woman want out of life? If you want to love and be loved, marriage offers the best opportunity to achieve your goal. Men may want, or think they want, a cafeteria selection of lunchcounter sex. But most women continue to want what the popular song calls "a Sunday kind of love." A happy marriage is the perfect vehicle for the Positive Woman. Marriage and motherhood give a woman new identity and the opportunity for all-round fulfillment as a woman.

Are you looking for security—emotional, social, financial? Nothing in this world is sure except death and taxes, but marriage and motherhood are the most reliable security the world can offer. . . .

Marriage and motherhood, of course, have their trials and tribulations. But what lifestyle doesn't? If you look upon your home as a cage, you will find yourself just as imprisoned in an office or a factory. The flight from the home is a flight from yourself, from responsibility, from the nature of woman, in pursuit of false hopes and fading illusions.

If you complain about servitude to a husband, servitude to a boss will be more intolerable. Everyone in the world has a boss of some kind. It is easier for most women to achieve a harmonious working relationship with a husband than with a foreman, supervisor, or office manager. . . .

If marriage is to be a successful institution, it must likewise have an ultimate decision maker, and that is the husband. Seen in this light, the laws that give the husband the right to establish the domicile of the marriage and to give his surname to his children are good laws designed to keep the family together. They are not anachronisms from a bygone era from which wives should be liberated in the name of equality.

Document E

Excerpts from "The Importance of Work"

(From Gloria Steinem, *Outrageous Acts and Everyday Rebellions*. New York: Holt, Rinehart and Winston, 1983, pp. 171–172.)

A job as a human right is a principle that applies to men as well as women. But women have more cause to fight for it. The phenomenon of the "working woman" has been held responsible for everything from an increase in male impotence (which turned out, incidentally, to be attributable to medication for high blood pressure) to the rising cost of steak (which was due to high energy costs and beef import restrictions, not women's refusal to prepare the cheaper, slower-cooking cuts). Unless we see a job as part of every citizen's right to autonomy and personal fulfillment, we will continue to be vulnerable to someone else's idea of what "need" is, and whose "need" counts the most.

In many ways, women who do not have to work for simple survival, but who choose to do so nonetheless, are on the frontier of asserting this right for all women. Those with well-to-do husbands are dangerously easy for us to resent and put down. It's easier still to resent women from families of inherited wealth, even though men generally control and benefit from that wealth. There is no Rockefeller Sister Fund, no J. P. Morgan and Daughters, and sons-in-law may be the ones who really sleep their way to power. But to prevent a woman whose husband or father is wealthy from earning her own living, and from gaining the self-confidence that comes with that ability, is to keep her needful of that unearned power and less willing to disperse it. Moreover, it is to lose forever her unique talent. . . .

For most of us, however, "women work because we have to" is just true enough to be seductive as a personal defense.

If we use it without also staking out the larger human right to a job, however, we will never achieve that right. And we will always be subject to the false argument that independence for women is a luxury affordable only in good economic times. Alternatives to layoffs will not be explored, acceptable unemployment will always be used to frighten those with jobs into accepting low wages, and we will never remedy the real cost, both to families and to the country, of dependent women and a massive loss of talent.

Worst of all, we may never learn to find productive, honored work as a natural part of ourselves and as one of life's basic pleasures.

Resources

Bibliography

Bell, Diane, and Renate Klein, eds. *Radically Speaking: Feminism Reclaimed.* North Melbourne, Australia: Spinifex Press, 1996.

Daniel, Robert L. *American Women in the Twentieth Century: The Festival of Life.* San Diego: Harcourt Brace Jovanovich, 1987.

Eisenstein, Zillah R. *The Radical Future of Liberal Feminism.* Boston: Northeastern University Press, 1981.

Felsenthal, Carol. *The Sweetheart of the Silent Majority: The Biography of Phyllis Schlafly.* Garden City, NY: Doubleday, 1981.

Friedan, Betty. *The Feminine Mystique.* New York: Norton, 1973.

Heilbrun, Carolyn G. *The Education of a Woman: The Life of Gloria Steinem.* New York: The Dial Press, 1995.

Linden-Ward, Blanche, and Carol Hurd Green. *Changing the Future: American Women in the 1960's.* New York: Twayne, 1993.

Klatch, Rebecca. *Women of the New Right.* Philadelphia: Temple University Press, 1987.

Norton, Mary Beth, and Ruth M. Alexander, eds. *Major Problems in American Women's History.* Lexington, MA: D.C. Heath, 1996.

Rosenberg, Rosalind. *Divided Lives: American Women in the 20th Century.* New York: Hill and Wang, 1992.

Schlafly, Phyllis. *The Power of the Positive Woman.* New Rochelle, NY: Arlington House Publishers, 1977.

Steinem, Gloria. *Outrageous Acts and Everyday Rebellions.* New York: Holt, Rinehart and Winston, 1983.

Steinem, Gloria. *Moving Beyond Words.* New York: Simon & Schuster, 1994.

Media Resources

Gloria Steinem, 50 minutes. Part of the Arts and Entertainment (A&E) series *Biography.* Available from http://www.biography.com/

Women in American Life—1955–1977. 25 minutes. National Women's History Project, 1988–1990. Reviews changes in the traditional family structure during the time frame considered. Available from Zenger Media, 800-421-4246.

The Women's Movement in the United States: An Interactive Encyclopedia. CD-ROM for Windows 95. Grades 7–12. Covers the history of the women's movement from colonial times to the present. Available from Zenger Media, 800-421-4246.

Teacher Guide

Key Features of Documents Used in This Book

Unit 1: Christopher Columbus and the New World

Document A is a letter from Columbus to Lord Sanchez. Columbus was attempting to explain encounters with the inhabitants of the lands he had discovered and claimed for Spain. Note how Columbus writes that he forbad the acceptance of valuable gifts from the natives in return for trinkets as being unjust. He himself gives valuable articles, but accepts nothing in return to win over their favor. He ultimately hopes that they will become Christians and accept the authority of Spain, while providing goods and materials that the mother country needs.

Bartolomé de las Casas (Document B) was a Franciscan monk who arrived in the New World to minister to the natives. His book *The Devastation of the Indies* is a classic work used to show the violence and cruelty of the Spanish to the native peoples. It became the foundation of the "Black Legend" that Spain's ultimate decline is divine punishment for Spanish treatment of the Indians. Note the publication date, which is many years after the voyages of Columbus. The illustrator of the book was Theodore de Bry, a Dutch engraver who had reason to paint the Spanish in as bad a light as possible due to the quarrels between Spain and the Low Countries.

Document C deals with the diseases unknowingly brought to the New World by the Europeans. This caused what has become known as a "virgin soil" epidemic, in which germs from the Old World infected New World peoples. They had not built up immunities to these diseases because of their years in isolation.

Document D is an illustration of a ceremony in which the heart of a human sacrifice is removed while still beating and offered to the sun god as a way of keeping the sun alive.

Document E describes an eyewitness account by a Spanish conquistador of an Aztec mass sacrifice of human victims for the sun god, Huitzilopouchtli. The Spanish were horrified by such scenes. Compare this document with Document B, the de las Casas account of Spanish cruelties and torture.

Unit 2: Samuel Adams and the American Revolution

Document A could be viewed as a powerful piece of colonial propaganda. The event is referred to as a "massacre," but while three people were killed and several were wounded, does this constitute our traditional view of a massacre? Note the closeness of the British soldiers and how they are portrayed as firing into the defenseless crowd at point-blank range. This kind of propaganda, the fear of public agitation, and Samuel Adams' forceful argument caused Governor Hutchinson to remove British troops from Boston and repeal the Townshend duties except for the tax on tea.

Document B is an eyewitness account of the Boston Tea Party. Note that the writer refers to the "Indians" as men of family and position in Boston. This was no unorganized rabble, but a well-planned event. Nothing was damaged except for the tea, and the ship was left in good condition.

Document C is an excerpt from the diary of John Adams reflecting on the Boston Tea Party. Adams believed that this movement was one of dignity and refers to the perpetrators as "Patriots," a significant appellation. Adams expresses concern over what actions the ministry will take in reaction to the Tea Party, but defends the colonists' destruction of the tea as absolutely necessary. To allow the tea to remain in the harbor, according to Adams, would mean giving up the right of no taxation without representation, something for which they had been fighting for ten years.

Document D gives the defense of the British government for the taxes levied upon the American colonies. George Grenville points out that when the Americans want the protection of Britain, they are quick to ask for it. The British nation has incurred a heavy debt to protect the Americans, and Grenville believes that it is only fair that the colonies contribute a small share of "the public expense." Grenville is concerned that the Americans' rebellious spirit has its roots in factions in Parliament and that the opposition is encouraging the colonists to believe that a more sympathetic party will gain power in the British government.

Document E gives the colonial governor's viewpoint of the rebellion. Governor Hutchinson viewed the colonial leaders as agitators who wished to involve the people as a whole in their desperate measures. He stated that the leadership was determined to gain their objectives, which required the participation of the entire body of the people to succeed. Once things had gone too far to back down, the consequence had to be an open revolt.

Unit 3: Andrew Jackson and the Removal of the Cherokee Nation

Document A is taken from Andrew Jackson's first annual message to Congress and gives his opinion as to the benefits of Indian removal. Jackson states that removing the tribes from the southeast will open territory to white settlers and not only allow a dense and civilized population to occupy the territory, but strengthen the frontier of the United States against any future invasions. States from which the Indians are removed will grow in wealth, population, and power. Removal will benefit the Indians as well because they will be separated from contact with whites and can rule themselves in their own way and become "civilized." Note Jackson's comments that removal of the Indians is part of progress—as one generation dies to make room for another, so must once-powerful tribes die out to make room for new peoples. Jackson states that no one would wish to see this country returned to the way it was when the forefathere founded it, covered with forests and inhabited by a few "savages."

Document B is from a letter by a Choctaw chief. The Choctaws were one of the tribes, along with the Cherokees, who were removed to "Indian Territory," present-day Oklahoma. Chief Harkins states that the removal is not a voluntary act and he fears what other acts may be done to his people. He pleads to have his people left alone. As they were friends when living east of the Mississippi, so will they remain friends in their present homeland, which he refers to as a "desert." Harkins hopes that if his tribe is oppressed again, there will be a public outcry against disturbing a sovereign people.

Document C is a speech before Congress made by David Crockett, congressman from the state of Tennessee. Crockett states that he is opposed to the removal of the Indians, even though he knows that his constituents are for it. He must follow his conscience for he believes that the Indian tribes are sovereign people and have been recognized by the United States government as such. Crockett is concerned about the condition of the land to which the tribes are being removed. He is concerned that the Indians are being driven from their land by force for the sole purpose of settling whites on former Indian lands.

Document D was written by Elias Boudinot, editor of the newspaper *The Cherokee Phoenix*. Boudinot is concerned that government officials have contended that the Indian tribes can never become civilized while surrounded by whites. He asks for evidence and proof that this assertion is true. Boudinot states that removal of a nation or tribe from civilization to the wilderness in order to be civilized is not something that has ever been done before.

In Document E, Wilson Lumpkin, the governor of Georgia, brings up memories of scalping Indians in his speech before Congress supporting Indian removal. Lumpkin denies that his state has been cruel to their native population, and he upholds Andrew Jackson as a "father to the Indians." The problem, according to Lumpkin, is that the rulers of the Cherokees are men who want power and do not wish to give up their sovereignty. He claims that the Indians who have already migrated west are happy with their new land and do not wish to return.

Unit 4: Lansford W. Hastings and the Donner Party

Document A is taken from Hastings' guidebook to California and Oregon. Note that it was written to attract settlers, particularly to California. Hastings describes the land in glowing terms. In the second part of the document cited, Hastings describes his new route to California. Note that he states that this new route is very good and much more direct. The Indians are timid and will not attack, and the streams are all able to be forded by wagons. Most emigrants had previously gone on the Oregon route and continued on to Oregon because it was a shorter and easier route. Hastings is trying to convince people that California, when using the new route, is the same distance from Independence, Missouri, as Oregon.

Document B is a letter written by one of the survivors, Virginia Reed, to her cousin back home. The spelling is the original. Note that Virginia states that Hastings told them that crossing the salt plain without water was only forty miles, but most of the survivors state that it was twice that long. They lost valuable animals and time. Virginia tells of getting stopped by the snow and eating whatever they could find, including their dog. The Reed family was able to survive without eating human flesh; according to Virginia, they were the only family who were able to get through without resorting to cannibalism. The last words of the letter are haunting: "never take no cutofs and hury along as fast as you can."

Document C was written by a member of the Harlan-Young Party, which took the Hastings Cutoff just ahead of the Donner Party. Note that the writer states that this was a very difficult route, particularly the desert portion, which necessitated resting the animals for three days. When their party arrived at the Humboldt River, they found that a party that had traveled the tried-and-true Fort Hall route was seventy miles ahead of them. The conclusion reached by the writer is that the fault lay in trying a new route and not taking the Fort Hall road, which was well known and well traveled.

Document D was written by H.A. Wise, who was what we would call today an adventure or travel writer. Wise tells the story of the Donner Party and totally blames them for their misfortune because of their ignorance and their loitering too many weeks on the route. His description of the cannibalism can only be compared to a modern "supermarket tabloid" and is greatly exaggerated. Wise remarks that emigrants must be prepared for hardship in making this rugged journey.

Document E was written by Jessy Quinn Thornton, an emigrant who traveled with the Donner Party until they split off to take the Hastings Cutoff to California. Thornton went on to Oregon, but took a new cutoff to Oregon which proved very difficult. Thornton states that Hastings assured the Donner Party that he had explored the new route and that it was much better than the old one via Fort Hall. He says that the road was generally easy to travel. Hastings claimed that the desert crossing was only 35 or 40 miles at the most. Thornton writes that upon meeting the survivors of the Donner Party in California, they asked him to publish this account in his journal.

Unit 5: Harriet Tubman and the Underground Railroad

Document A consists of excerpts from the United States Constitution concerned with issues of indenture and slavery. These sections of the Constitution represent the manner in which the Founding Fathers dealt with the "peculiar institution" of slavery. They formed the basis for the legal treatment of slaves in the United States before the Civil War. They also pertain to concerns of the Federal Government such as taxation, representation (in so far as the seats in the House of Representatives of the Congress are determined by the populations of the respective states), the ability of individual states to pass laws with respect to slavery, international trade, and interstate commerce. It is important to note that, at the Constitutional Convention, Northern delegates insisted that an indentured servant or slave be counted as three-fifths of a free person, while Southern delegates wanted them counted as whole persons in order to maximize their representation (and therefore their ability to control legislation concerning slavery) in Congress. Article IV, Section 2, was superseded by the Thirteenth Amendment.

Document B is an excerpt from Harriet Beecher Stowe's 1852 novel, *Uncle Tom's Cabin, or, Life Among the Lowly*. Born in Connecticut, Stowe (1811–1896) was both the daughter and wife of prominent Congregationalist clergymen. Reflecting her revulsion against slavery on both moral and religious grounds, her novel, serialized in 1851 and adapted for the stage shortly after its publication as a novel, raised the level of indignation about slavery in the north in the decade before the Civil War and became a major element of abolitionist propaganda.

Document C is part of the congressional act passed in 1793 to create a procedure to be followed in returning runaway slaves to their masters. It left the recapture of runaways to the slave owners or their agents, but provided that such seizures could take place anywhere in the United States and imposed a fine on those convicted of aiding runaways or interfering with their recapture.

Document D consists of excerpts from the Fugitive Slave Act passed in 1850 to amend the 1793 law. Faced with increasing numbers of runaways and a growing movement to assist them, Congress, as part of the Compromise of 1850, moved to increase the role of federal authorities in the recapture of runaway slaves to increase the penalties against those who harbored or assisted them.

Exhibit E includes excerpts from the U.S. Supreme Court's 1857 "Dred Scott Decision." Dred Scott was a slave who, in 1834, was taken north by his master from Missouri, a slave state (so defined by the Missouri Compromise of 1820), into the free state of Illinois and thence to the free territory of Wisconsin. Once back in Missouri, Scott sued for his freedom, based on the assertion that his residence in free states and territories erased his slave status. Missouri argued that, as a slave, Scott was not a citizen and therefore had no right to sue for redress through the federal courts. In making its decision, the Supreme Court majority not only agreed with the State, but went on to argue that Congress had exceeded its authority under the Constitution when it excluded slavery from the northern states under the Missouri and 1850 Compromises. The decision (along with the passage of the Kansas–Nebraska Act three years earlier) seemed to many to confirm the view that legislative compromises over the issue of slavery were no longer possible.

Document F is an account by William Still, a Philadelphia agent for the Underground Railroad who was involved in hundreds of escapes and was present when Henry Brown completed his journey north in a baize-lined container. It shows the lengths to which slaves would go to escape to freedom. After Brown's escape was publicized, southern shippers and freight handlers became much more attentive in their inspections of boxes and crates shipped north.

Unit 6: Sitting Bull and the "Pacification" of the Western Indian Tribes

Document A is a poem by Walt Whitman commemorating Custer's death. Note how Custer is portrayed as a hero, almost a martyr figure.

Document B is the viewpoint of an Indian woman who was in a nearby village when the United States cavalry attacked just before the final Battle of Little Bighorn. Mrs. Spotted Horn Bull states that the Indians had not planned to attack the soldiers—this was not a premeditated act, but self-defense. She states that the warriors had not anticipated this fight, but reacted to the soldiers attacking first.

Document C is taken from a speech made by Chief Red Cloud to the U.S. secretary of the interior in 1870. Red Cloud signed the Treaty of Laramie, but later felt that he had been deceived by the U.S. government. In this document, Red Cloud states that the government has made many promises which it is not keeping. Red Cloud does not wish to leave his homeland and move to another territory. The chief states that he does not want war with the government, but asks the secretary to tell the Great Father (president of the United States) that he feels betrayed and cheated.

Document D is an excerpt from the Fort Laramie Treaty with the Lakota Sioux, signed in 1868. Note that both the Indians and the United States government pledge to maintain peace. Note that the government promises to provide education for the Indians, which, as Red Cloud complained in the last document, is not provided. Article 16 of the treaty stipulates Dakota Territory as Indian territory and states that no white person should be allowed to settle there or pass through without permission of the Sioux.

Document E is an excerpt from a book written by Libby Custer to memorialize her husband and their life together. Libby clearly blames Sitting Bull for refusing to make a treaty with the government and move to a reservation. She, very emotionally, recounts the story of how the women at the fort received the word of the fateful day at Little Bighorn.

Unit 7: William McKinley and the Spanish-American War

Document A is the transcript of an informal talk that President McKinley gave to a delegation of Methodist clergymen explaining how he came to the conclusion to annex the Philippines in the wake of the U.S. victory in the Spanish-American War. It lays out the alternatives the president considered and shows the imperialist ambition, racial prejudice, and religious conviction that colored his thinking.

Document B is an American translation of the declaration made by rebel leader and provisional Filipino President Emilio Aguinaldo upon hearing that American forces had begun their occupation of Luzon. It helps us to understand that he regarded the Philippines as a nation that the United States had helped to set free from Spain.

Document C is a speech on the Senate floor by Democratic South Carolina Senator Benjamin "Pitchfork" Tillman questioning the morality of the Philippine annexation. It is a clear statement of the anti-imperialist position. Tillman was a southern populist politician, supported by the Farmers' Alliance, who served in the Senate from 1895 until his death in 1918.

Document D contains excerpts from the report of a U.S. presidential commission, appointed to set forth justifications and goals for the U.S. occupation.

Poet and novelist Rudyard Kipling (born in India in 1865, died in England in 1936) glorified the expansion of the British Empire—and, by implication, that of other European powers (including the U.S.)—at the end of the nineteenth century. He was the first English writer to win the Nobel Prize (in 1907). His 1899 poem "The White Man's Burden," Document E, is the clearest embodiment of the justification for such imperialism.

Document F is a Senate speech setting forth the goal for the American occupation by Massachusetts Republican Senator Henry Cabot Lodge (1850–1924). A senator since 1894, Lodge was a valued advisor to Theodore Roosevelt, who became president when McKinley was assassinated in 1901. He would eventually become the chairman of the Foreign Relations Committee and majority leader in the Senate.

Unit 8: Henry Ford and the American Worker

Document A contains excerpts from Henry Ford's 1922 autobiography justifying his manner of organizing production and his expectations toward those who worked for him.

Document B is an account of his company's extension of these modes of production to the airframe manufacturing industry (up to then more of a handicraft industry) during World War II at the Ford Willow Run Plant.

Document C demonstrates some of the negative effects of Ford's method of manufacturing. American author John Dos Passos (1896–1970) wrote *The Big Money*, his socially radical and stylistically innovative 1936 novel, about the corruption of the 1920s and the crash that followed. *The Big Money* is the final part of his *U.S.A. Trilogy*; the first two parts are *The 42nd Parallel* (1930), set in the period before World War I, and *1919* (1932), about the wartime experience. Biographies of real people, like Ford, "newsreels" describing actual events, and "camera eye" point-of-view segments are interspersed throughout the trilogy's story line that follows a fictional cast of characters through three decades of American history.

Document D is automobile historian James K. Flink's generally (though not completely) positive summary of the larger economic, social, and cultural impacts of "automobility" on the United States.

Documents E and F present challenges to this view by architecture historian and critic Jane Holtz Kay and by social critic Ivan Illich.

Unit 9: Elizabeth Gurley Flynn and the Radical Labor Movement

Document A contains excerpts from an essay written by Flynn during the 1913 Industrial Workers of the World-supported textile workers' strike in Paterson, New Jersey, and published two years later by the Cleveland, Ohio, IWW chapter. The words are supposedly from a transcript of a speech on the subject given by Flynn (the pamphlet was later withdrawn and the Cleveland chapter dissolved). The use of sabotage as a tactic in labor's war against industrial corporations was controversial, even among Wobblies themselves. Anarchists demanded that it be openly adopted and criticized the IWW for not doing so. At the same time, the failure to denounce its use was the issue that caused the Socialist Party to expel IWW leader "Big" Bill Haywood in 1912. Flynn expressed her own doubts about its universal application in a 1916 letter to President Woodrow Wilson, but wrote the pamphlet to support New York Socialist Frederic Sumner Boyd, who had been arrested during the strike and sentenced to five years in prison for advocating sabotage. By the time the pamphlet was printed, Boyd had petitioned for pardon by renouncing its use, which Flynn denounced as a cowardly act on the pamphlet's last page. The pamphlet was placed into her FBI file and was used as evidence against her both in her 1951 Smith Act trial and in a 1952 Subversive Activities Control Board meeting. It is important both for itself and as an example of the kind of almost 40-year-old evidence that was used to prove her dangerous in the early years of the Cold War.

Document B is a 1926 testimonial letter from labor leader and American Socialist Party head Eugene V. Debs praising Flynn's efforts on behalf of labor. Eugene Victor Debs (1855–1926) was a leader of the Brotherhood of Locomotive Engineers. He was present in 1905 at the founding of the IWW and was the titular head and perennial presidential candidate of the Socialist Party. Debs was tried under the Espionage Act for his opposition to American entry into World War I. Sent to prison in 1919, he ran again for president and received one million votes. On Christmas Day 1921, President Harding pardoned him and ordered his release. He died shortly after writing this letter in support of Flynn.

Document C is an excerpt from the Smith Act. Proposed as one of a number of antisubversive measures by Virginia Congressman Howard W. Smith, it was absorbed, in modified form, as Title I of the Alien Registration Act passed in 1940 as part of the United States' growing preparedness for, and nervousness about, the war that had broken out in Europe in September 1939 (and was taken advantage of by Nazi Germany's Axis partner, Japan, as it expanded into Southeast Asia). Section I of the Title provided penalties for anyone attempting to undermine military morale, while Sections II and III did the same for anyone advocating the violent overthrow of the government or joining an organization with this as a purpose. Other Titles of the act required the registration and fingerprinting of all aliens in the country. Title I was used in 1941 to indict Socialist Workers Party members in Minnesota, but was rarely invoked during World War II (when the Soviet Union was one of the United Nations fighting the Axis). As the Cold War emerged, the Smith Act became a primary tool in the war against domestic Communists. Though it was never repealed, Supreme Court decisions since the early '60s have sharply limited definitions of prohibited acts and have invalidated its use to stifle criticism of the government and limit other civil liberties.

Document D is an excerpt from the prosecution cross-examination of Flynn during the *United States* v.

Flynn prosecution of 12 members of the U.S. Communist Party for violation of Title I of the Smith Act. It provides insight into her reasons for joining the Communist Party.

Document E is Flynn's reaction to that prosecution.

Unit 10: Fred Korematsu and Japanese Interment

Documents A and B are the Federal law and Executive Order permitting the Secretary of War to create, by executive order, military zones or areas inside the United States and to establish penalties for anyone acting in ways proscribed by regulations issued within those zones.

Documents C and D are orders issued by the Western Defense Command excluding "persons of Japanese ancestry, both alien and non-alien" from the San Francisco Bay area (similar orders were issued all along the West Coast) and establishing the steps through which the evacuation would take place.

It is important to note that General Delos Emmons, the military governor of Hawaii, resisted all efforts to exclude the 160,000 Japanese Americans living there, interning only 1,444 persons—979 aliens and 525 citizens—for security reasons. No acts of espionage or sabotage occurred there during the war. After Pearl Harbor, Roosevelt asked Chicago businessman Curtis Munson to gather information about the loyalty of Japanese living in the United States. His report, as well as those of the Office of Naval Intelligence and the Federal Bureau of Investigation, concluded that all suspected individuals were already in custody and that there was no security justification for the removal of Japanese Americans from the West Coast. Initially, the U.S. Department of Justice refused General DeWitt's request for authority to search Japanese Americans without probable cause.

Document E is a Department of Justice justification of the relocations.

Document F was written as an English class assignment by a Japanese-American evacuee. It was written at the Tule Lake Relocation Center, just south of the California-Oregon border, where Yoshikawa and his family were sent from their home in Oregon.

Documents G, H, I, and J are excerpts of the U.S. Supreme Court decisions on the Japanese internment. Despite concerns felt by individual Justices that the internment violated the Constitution's Equal Protection clause, in 1943 the Court found unanimously in favor of the government's wartime emergency powers in *Hirabayashi* (Document G) and *Yasui* (Document H), upheld the government in a split decision in 1944 in *Korematsu* (Document J), and later that same year found against the government in *Endo* (Document I).

Document K is an excerpt from the 1988 restitution act passed by the U.S. Congress.

Unit 11: Harry S. Truman and the Dropping of the Atomic Bomb

Document A is the memorandum prepared by Secretary of War Henry Stimson and Manhattan District* director General Leslie Groves to introduce newly inaugurated President Harry Truman to the bomb and its potential. Truman had no knowledge of the bomb project (though as a senator, he had voted its funds) before President Roosevelt died on April 12, 1945. Note the various contexts into which these men placed the bomb as they oriented the president about its existence.

Document B is the Franck Report, submitted to the government in June 1945, arguing against the use of the bomb against Japan. James Franck was a German émigré chemist who had won a Nobel Prize in 1925 and was working on photosynthesis at the University of Chicago. Arthur Compton (Nobel Prize laureate, head of the nuclear reaction project at the University of Chicago, and younger brother of M.I.T. president and Interim Committee member Karl Compton) recruited Franck in 1942 to direct the Manhattan District's Metallurgical Laboratory chemistry section. Franck agreed to do so on condition that, before any decision was made to use the bomb, he would be given the opportunity to express his views to the nation's leaders. After the bomb's use had been recommended on May 31 by the Interim Committee (only General Marshall, present as a guest, spoke against its use), Compton (who had voted in favor of its use) remembered his promise to Franck, returned to Chicago, and asked him to set up a Committee on Social and Political Implications to express the scientists' views. Franck, along with Leo Szilard and Eugene R. Rabinowitch, prepared this seven-page memorandum, and Franck went back to Washington with Compton to present it to the government. Compton was asked to submit the report to the Scientific Panel of the Interim Committee (he described it to its members at a meeting at Los Alamos in mid-June) and then report its views to the Committee itself. On June 21, 1945, without actually seeing the report, the Interim Committee reaffirmed its recommendation that the bomb be used against Japan.

Document C is a selection of the notes taken by the Interim Committee's recording secretary, J. Gordon Arneson, at one of the Committee's meetings as the decisions about how to use the bomb were made. The choice of which cities to bomb fell to Secretary Stimson, who received advice from a targeting committee of Army Air Force officers appointed by General Groves. Stimson rejected the committee's first choice, Kyoto, because of its cultural and historic significance and its lack of important military installations.

Document D is the bombing order issued to United States Army Air Force Strategic bombing commander, General Spaatz, on July 25, 1945.

Document E contains entries in President Truman's diary from the period of the Potsdam Conference as Truman informed Stalin about the bomb and the Soviet reaction to that information. (Note that Stalin's agents had infiltrated the Manhattan District and that Soviet scientists, led by Igor Vasilevich Kurchatov, were already working on a Soviet bomb project.)

Documents F and G contain extracts from the notes of Soviet Foreign Minister Molotov and from the memoirs of Marshal Zhukov. They make clear that Stalin was well aware of the possibility of a U.S. atomic bomb and that the Soviets were preparing their own as quickly as possible.

Document H is the Potsdam Declaration broadcast to the Japanese at the end of the Potsdam Conference.

Document I is an account of the impact of the bomb on the Hiroshima population.

Document J is President Truman's announcement to the American people on the use of the bomb. Note that the name of the city bombed is missing to permit insertion of an alternate target if weather conditions prevented the bombing of Hiroshima.

Document K is the excerpt of President Truman's 1955 memoir about his decision to use the bomb. Note his forceful and narrow justification of its use, which has remained controversial ever since.

Unit 12: César Chávez and Migrant Farm Workers

Document A is a speech given by Chávez during a 250-mile Easter march from Delano, California, where a prolonged and bitter strike by Hispanic (largely Mexican) grape workers was taking place, to the state capital (Sacramento) to dramatize the plight of migrant farm workers. Note the connections to traditional belief that Chávez makes to motivate the marchers.

Document B consists of extracts from the decision of a California Appeals Court to overturn César Chávez's conviction by a local court in a rural district for violating an ordinance prohibiting the use of car-mounted loudspeakers on county roads. Since the union had been denied access to farm workers by the owners of the property where they worked, Chávez used these loudspeakers to communicate with them from county roads adjacent to the fields.

Document C contains César Chávez's memories of the early days of the economic boycott that the National Farm Workers Association* organized to support "La Causa"—their fight to organize impover-

---

* The code name for the project to develop the atomic bomb—its official designation was S-1.

* The National Farm Workers Association joined with an American Federation of Labor affiliate in 1966 to form the United Farm Workers.

ished and largely (legally) unprotected migrant farm laborers who worked for California vineyards. Later the group expanded to help vegetable farmers and agribusinesses.

Document D is the text of a speech given on Martin Luther King's birthday in 1990 by César Chávez. Chávez was paying tribute to the civil rights leader and the lessons he taught others (including Chávez) who were struggling for social justice.

Document E lists a series of inspirational quotes from César Chávez's life and work, compiled by the César E. Chávez Foundation.

Unit 13: Gloria Steinem and the Women's Movement

Document A is from a speech given at the Smith College graduation of 1954. Note how the role of the graduates is portrayed. They are wished a "happy marriage" because that is to be their "supreme role."

Document B is from a book that really rocked the traditional view of women's roles and attitudes, *The Feminine Mystique* by Betty Friedan. Friedan writes about the ideal fulfillment of the American woman—to be a perfect wife and mother—and how this may not be enough for many women.

Jerry Falwell was a founder of the "Moral Majority" and is an opponent of the feminist movement. In Document C, Falwell gives his views on the role of women, which he believes is God-given. Falwell believes that the Equal Rights Amendment will strike at the foundation of American society and actually rob women of the special status they enjoy as being honored by their husbands. Falwell declares that according to scripture, women are weaker than men, but are still important and honored by their husbands.

Document D is an excerpt from a book by Phyllis Schlafly, a conservative who opposed the feminist movement. According to Schlafly, a "Positive Woman" can find all the identity and fulfillment she needs in a happy marriage. Marriage and motherhood provide the best kind of security, and in pursuing a career, a woman is simply running away from responsibility and the true nature of woman.

Document E is an excerpt from an article by Gloria Steinem titled "The Importance of Work." Steinem argues that a job is a human right for all people, regardless of gender. She decries the way that women entering the work force have been blamed for all sorts of societal woes, including the rising cost of steak. Steinem wants the right to a job not tied to economic times or the status of the person seeking a job, but to be guaranteed as a right for all humans. Steinem sees productive and honored work as something natural to women and one of life's pleasures.

Grading Rubric for Document-Based Essays

- Student has a clear thesis statement in an introductory paragraph.
- Student uses a majority of the documents in making his or her arguments.
- Student supports thesis with appropriate evidence from the documents.
- Student has an understanding of the content of the documents.
- Documents are quoted or cited correctly.
- Student is able to detect and analyze bias or point of view in at least two of the documents.
- Student is able to bring in appropriate outside historical information from the background material provided and the suggested readings.
- Student has a good concluding paragraph that sums up the thesis and the evidence for its veracity.

Mock Trials

- STUDENT INFORMATION SHEETS
- GUIDEPOST ACTIVITIES
- WITNESS LIST

Courtroom Personnel and Their Roles

Name of Personnel: **Student Taking Role:**

Defendant

Person charged with a crime. Presumed to be innocent until   _____
proven guilty beyond a reasonable doubt.

Judge

Conducts the trial and maintains order. Recognizes the attor-   _____
neys for the defense and prosecution and keeps the order of the
trial flowing correctly. May rule on whether evidence is admis-
sible if it is questioned by an attorney.

Court Clerk

Aids the judge in conducting the trial. Calls the court to order   _____
as the judge enters by saying, "All rise. Superior Court of the
State of _____, in the County of _____, the Honorable
Judge _____ presiding, is now in session. Please be seated
and come to order." The clerk also swears in witnesses: "You do
solemnly affirm that the testimony you may give in the case
now pending before this court shall be the truth, the whole
truth, and nothing but the truth."

Bailiff

The bailiff brings in the defendant and is responsible for the se-   _____
curity of the proceedings. The bailiff also brings in the witnesses to testify as they are called.

Attorneys

Attorneys argue their side of the case and present evidence and
call witnesses. They should not supply information on their
own, but use witnesses and evidence to prove their case.

Prosecuting Attorney(s)

The prosecuting attorney tries to convince the judge or jury   _____
that the defendant is guilty beyond a reasonable doubt.

_____

Critical Thinking Using
Primary Sources in U.S. History

Name of Personnel:	**Student Taking Role:**

Defense Attorney(s)

The defense attorney presents the case on behalf of the defendant and tries to disprove the prosecution's case. Defense attempts to undermine the prosecution's case by showing that the witnesses cannot be depended upon or that the evidence is questionable. Defense attorneys particularly look for inconsistencies in testimony.

Witnesses

Witnesses supply the facts in the case. They may state only facts, not opinions. The attorneys will watch for this. Witnesses may be called by either the prosecution or the defense. They may be called because of their expertise in a particular field relating to the evidence, or if they were eyewitnesses to a pivotal event relating to the charges against the defendant. They may also be called as character witnesses for the defendant.

The Jury

The role of the jury is to listen to all the facts of the case as presented by the prosecution and defense. The jury must then decide whether the defendant is guilty or not guilty of the crime. It may base its decision only on the facts presented during the trial and not on any outside sources or knowledge. Traditionally, there are twelve people on a jury, but for this trial, you may use a different number, depending upon the number of participating students.

> **Note** on the jury: Rather than use members of your own class as jurors, you may wish to have another class act as the jury, or you may wish to use parents or teachers as jurors.

Trial Procedure and Glossary of Legal Terms

There are four main stages to a trial: Opening Statements, Direct Examination of the Witnesses, Cross-Examination of the Witnesses, and Closing Arguments.

I.   Opening Statements
1. Opening statement by the prosecution
2. Opening statement by the defense (The defense attorney may decide to present her opening statement after the prosecution presents its entire case.)

II. Prosecution Presents Its Case (This procedure is repeated until the prosecution has called all of its witnesses.)
1. Prosecution calls first witness and goes through the direct examination of the witness.
2. Defense attorney cross-examines prosecution's first witness.
3. (optional) Prosecution may examine its witness again to clarify issues brought up by the defense.
4. (optional) Defense may cross-examine prosecution's witness again.

III. Defense Presents Its Case (This procedure is repeated until the defense has called all of its witnesses.)
1. Defense calls first witness and goes through the direct examination of this witness.
2. Prosecution cross-examines defense's first witness.
3. (optional) Defense may examine its witness again to clarify issues brought up by prosecution.
4. (optional) Prosecution may cross-examine defense's witness again.

IV. Closing Arguments
1. Closing argument by the prosecution
2. Closing argument by the defense

Legal Terms:

Affidavit: A written declaration made under oath before an official such as a notary or court personnel.

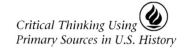

Critical Thinking Using
Primary Sources in U.S. History

Closing argument: Each side presents a summation of its case. The summation reviews the testimony heard, the evidence brought forward, and the arguments made by counsel. This is given in the past tense, as in "The prosecution has shown that. . ." or "Evidence has proven that. . . . "

Counsel: A formal term for a lawyer (or group of lawyers), particularly an attorney conducting a case in court.

Cross-examination: Questioning that occurs after the direct examination and is conducted by the counsel who did not call this witness.

Deposition: A written statement under oath by a witness for use in court, particularly if the witness cannot appear.

Direct examination: The first questioning of the witness by the counsel who called the witness to the stand.

Objection: What occurs when an attorney believes that the opposing attorney has violated the rules of evidence. The attorney may feel that the evidence presented is not relevant to the issues of the case, or that a question is leading, ambiguous, or based upon hearsay. It is then up to the judge to decide whether the objection has merit ("Objection sustained") or not ("Objection overruled").

Opening statement: When counsel, either prosecution or defense, presents an outline or summary of their case. The opening statement is a presentation of the issues and arguments that will be shown during the course of the trial and is always made in the future tense, such as "The defense will demonstrate. . . " or "Evidence will prove that. . . ."

Plaintiff: The party that institutes the suit in court; tends to be used more in civil trials than in criminal trials.

Testimony: The affirmation of fact or truth as given before a court, usually done orally, as in the "testimony given by a witness."

Looking at the Evidence

For each case, you will receive evidence in the form of "documents." These are rather like the "exhibits" used as evidence in a trial. Here, evidence can be a primary source or a secondary source. A primary source is a document or an artifact that is from the time period you are concerned with. For example, a letter from Christopher Columbus about one of his voyages is a primary source document. A sculpture from early-sixteenth-century Mesoamerica is an example of a primary source artifact. A secondary source is generally a written document, such as a textbook or magazine article, written by historians or other specialists based on their research.

Using sources, particularly primary sources, can be compared to acting as a detective sleuthing through history. You need to question the evidence, evaluate it, and draw inferences or conclusions based upon your careful analysis. It is important to view each piece of evidence with a critical eye. As a member of either the prosecution or defense team, you will wish to point out the truth of the evidence you use and "poke holes" in the evidence used by opposing counsel.

Keep the following things in mind when examining the evidence in each case:

- What kind of evidence is this? A document? An artifact? A primary or secondary source?
- If the evidence is a written document, what kind of document is it? A private letter, a public proclamation, a government dispatch?
- Who wrote or produced this evidence?
- Why was this document written or this artifact produced? Think of underlying motives!
- For whom was this document or artifact produced?
- When was it produced? How far removed is it from the event with which it is concerned?
- Where was the evidence constructed or written?
- If this is a secondary source, who wrote it, and what are his or her credentials?
- Can this piece of evidence be verified in any way? Is there another piece of evidence that corroborates it?

Critical Thinking Using
Primary Sources in U.S. History

Opening Statement

Opening Statement for the Prosecution

The purpose is to inform the jury of the facts of the case. There will be no argument, discussion of law, or objections by the defense attorney or the defendant during your opening statements.

You should give: The name of the case, your name, your client's name (in the historical cases, the "people" may be the client; as in criminal cases, the "state" is who the prosecution is working for), the name of the defendant, the name of the defendant's counsel, a description or story of the facts in the case, a summary of the key facts that witnesses will bring forth in testimony, importance of any evidence/documents to be used in the case, and a strong conclusion that the guilt of the accused will be proved.

Opening Statement for the Defense

The purpose of your opening statement is to deny that the prosecution has a valid case and to briefly outline the facts from the defendant's point of view. There will be no interruptions or arguments from the prosecution during your opening statements.

You should give: Your name and your client's name (that of the defendant), a general synopsis of the defense, facts that tend to weaken the prosecution's case, a summary of what each defense witness will testify to, and a strong conclusion that the innocence of the accused will be maintained.

Your Opening Statement:

_____

_____

_____

_____

_____

_____

_____

_____

_____

Witnesses

Both prosecution and defense will wish to call witnesses. In the direct examination of a witness, the purpose is to present evidence that will get the verdict your side wishes to achieve. You should try to clearly present the facts to convince the jury of the logic of your case. You should also try to present your witnesses to the greatest advantage by demonstrating their credibility. Avoid complex questions; keep them clear and simple. Ask open-ended questions, which usually begin with "what," "who," "where," "when," or "how." You should take notes when the witnesses called by opposing counsel give testimony so that you can cross-examine those witnesses. The purpose of cross-examination is to discredit your opponent's witness. Plan what witnesses *you* will call and some potential questions.

Witness: **Possible Questions:**

_____   _____

_____   _____

_____   _____

_____   _____

_____   _____

_____   _____

_____   _____

_____   _____

_____   _____

_____   _____

Critical Thinking Using
Primary Sources in U.S. History

Witness Affidavit

As a witness in a trial, you will be called upon to give a truthful account of issues and events pertaining to the case. In order to prepare for your court appearance, you should write down pertinent information in the form of a narrative. Include your name, your occupation, where you live, how long you have known the defendant (if at all), and any dealings you have had with the defendant. If you are an expert witness (e.g., doctor, handwriting analyst, ecologist, military tactician) who will be called upon to give testimony about an aspect of the case, try to guess the questions you will be asked by either the defense or the prosecution. Provide possible answers in your narrative.

_____

_____

_____

_____

_____

_____

_____

_____

_____

_____

_____

_____

_____

_____

_____

_____

Evidence Information

Both the defense and prosecution teams will need to make use of evidence to prove their cases. Use this sheet to make notes on the evidence provided (Documents A, B, C, D, and E, etc.), as well as any other evidence you may uncover in your research. Think about how you can use this evidence to prove the guilt or innocence of the defendant.

Exhibit:	Notes:

Closing Arguments

You cannot really formulate your closing argument until you have heard all of the testimony. A few members of your team can begin working on the closing argument as the last witnesses are being called. Remember—the closing argument reviews the testimony heard, the evidence brought forward, and the arguments made by counsel. Use this sheet to set down your closing argument. Use the past tense, as in "Defense has demonstrated. . . " or "Prosecution has proved that. . . ."

_____

_____

_____

_____

_____

_____

_____

_____

_____

_____

_____

_____

_____

_____

_____

_____

_____

_____

Newspaper Account of the Trial

Court trials seem to be items of great interest in the media. Some courts allow live media coverage; some allow representatives from the print and video media to be present, but with no live coverage permitted. Your challenge is to write a news report of the trial in which you have participated. You may write a report for one of the following news sources: a local newspaper, *The New York Times,* a news magazine, or a tabloid. Think of who your readership might be while writing your report. Observe the proper journalistic practice of explaining the "who," "what," "where," "when," "how," and "why." Don't forget the headline!

_____

_____

_____

_____

_____

_____

_____

_____

_____

_____

_____

_____

_____

_____

_____

_____

Witness List: Other Historical Figures Connected with Each Unit

If you decide to use the documents to construct a simulated trial, these are "witnesses" who might be called.

Unit 1: Christopher Columbus and the New World

Francisco de Bobadilla: Royal governor of Santo Domingo who arrested Columbus and deported him to Spain in 1500.

Theodore de Bry: Dutch publisher and engraver working in Germany who created many of the pictures of the New World and portrayals of the Native Americans in the early 1500s.

Bartolomé de las Casas: Spanish missionary who protested the treatment of the natives of the New World.

Bartholomé Colón: Brother of Christopher Columbus who helped plan and organize the voyages to the New World.

Guacanagari: The cacique, or leader, of the Arawak tribes in northwestern Hispaniola (present-day Haiti).

Queen Isabella: Ruler of Castile who married King Ferdinand of Aragon. Together they conquered the last Muslim enclave and united Spain as a Catholic country. Isabella provided the financial backing for Columbus' voyages westward to the "Indies."

Nicholas de Ovando: Governor of the Indies as of 1501, who replaced Columbus.

Martin Pinzon: Shipbuilder who provided vessels for Columbus' first expedition and captained the *Pinta*.

Tainos: The "Indians" who inhabited the Caribbean islands first encountered by Columbus.

Unit 2: Samuel Adams and the American Revolution

John Adams: Second cousin of Samuel Adams, a Boston lawyer who defended the British soldiers involved in the "Boston Massacre" and who became one of the leaders of the Revolution. He served as a diplomat in the 1780s, as the first vice president of the United States, and as the second president.

Thomas Hutchinson: Native of Massachusetts who served as British royal governor of the colony in the crisis years leading up to the Revolution.

Lord Frederick North: British Tory Prime Minister appointed in 1770, who bowed to the wishes of King George III and tried to keep the colonies in line with British mercantilist policies.

Thomas Paine: Writer of *Common Sense*, a popular pamphlet advocating the Revolution. He became disillusioned with its outcome, supported the French Revolution, was imprisoned by the Jacobins, and spent his last years in the United States in poverty.

William Pitt (the younger): Member of the Whig opposition party in the British Parliament who opposed the taxes levied on the colonies. His father, William Pitt, the Earl of Chatham, had been prime minister during the French and Indian War. Pitt the younger became prime minister at the end of the American Revolution.

Paul Revere: Businessman and silversmith who became a leading figure in the revolutionary movement in Boston.

Sons of Liberty: An organization of American colonists formed in opposition to the 1765 Stamp Act. The group participated in the Boston Tea Party and other acts of intimidation and rebellion against British policies and colonial authorities.

Charles Townshend: Tory leader of the House of Commons and author of the Townshend Acts, which imposed taxes and asserted parliamentary authority over the colonies.

Unit 3: Andrew Jackson and the Removal of the Cherokee Nation

Elias Boudinot: Editor of the Cherokee newspaper *The Weekly Phoenix*. He supported the removal treaty, was fired in 1832, and was later murdered.

Martin Van Buren: Head of the Democratic Party in New York and friend of Andrew Jackson. He occupied various positions in Jackson's administration and succeeded him as president.

Critical Thinking Using
Primary Sources in U.S. History

John C. Calhoun: A native of South Carolina and strong defender of slavery. He served as Jackson's first vice president and was his rival within the Democratic Party.

George Guess (Sequoyah): Inventor of a written language for the Cherokees as a means of asserting their identity.

Wilson Lumpkin: Governor of Georgia and vocal supporter of Indian removal. He equated support for Indian rights with an attack on slavery.

Wilma Mankiller: A vocal spokesperson for Indian rights in the 1970s. She became the first woman chief of a Native American tribe when she was elected chief of the Cherokees in 1988.

John Marshall: U.S. Supreme Court Chief Justice who ruled that the Cherokees were a domestic dependent state over which the federal government had exclusive jurisdiction.

Major Ridge: Cherokee and member of the so-called "treaty party" of the tribe that favored removal.

John Ross: Leader of the Cherokee national party that opposed the tribe's move from Georgia.

Winfield Scott: Capable soldier (called "Old Fuss and Feathers" by his troops) and rival to Jackson during his military service. General Scott believed that Jackson engaged in military excesses. He supervised the Cherokee removal from Georgia.

Daniel Webster: Leader of the Whig opposition party in Congress.

Unit 4: Lansford W. Hastings and the Donner Party

Patrick Breen: Irishman, member of the Donner Party, and one of its few survivors.

Jim Bridger: Trapper who ran a fort located in the foothills of the Sierras for trade with parties on their way to California.

Edwin Bryant: Member of the Donner Party who went ahead of the main group and tried to warn the party against the Hastings Cutoff.

James Clyman: "Mountain man" familiar with the Oregon trail and the Hastings Cutoff area.

John C. Fremont: Explorer who investigated the mountains in California and declared California part of the United States in 1845. In 1850, he was elected a senator from California and in 1856 became the Republican Party's first presidential candidate.

Lewis Keseberg: Another survivor of the Donner Party, best known for his involvement with cannibalism in the pass.

C.F. McGlashan: Author of a history of the Donner Party in the late 1800s that unearthed much of what we know about the tragedy.

James Reed: Member of the Donner Party who survived the ordeal because he was banished from the group and sent ahead after causing the death of another party member. He later led the relief effort to reach the Donner Party in the Sierras.

Virginia Reed: James Reed's stepdaughter and survivor of the Donner Party expedition.

John Sutter: California land speculator and settler who helped to organize a Donner relief effort. Later, gold was found on his property, triggering the 1848–49 gold rush.

Unit 5: Harriet Tubman and the Underground Railroad

James Buchanan: President of the United States prior to the Civil War. As chief executive he was responsible for the enforcement of the Fugitive Slave Law.

Frederick Douglass: Former slave and famous abolitionist orator.

Stephen A. Douglas: Democratic party leader and writer of the Fugitive Slave Law who supported slave owners' rights. He is best known for his series of debates with Abraham Lincoln.

William Lloyd Garrison: Abolitionist writer and newspaper publisher who supported the efforts of the Underground Railroad.

Harriet Beecher Stowe: Author of the antislavery novel *Uncle Tom's Cabin.*

Roger Taney: Supreme Court Chief Justice who wrote the majority opinion upholding the legality of the Fugitive Slave Law.

Critical Thinking Using
Primary Sources in U.S. History

Unit 6: Sitting Bull and the "Pacification" of the Western Indian Tribes

Crazy Horse: Commander of the Sioux side of the Battle of Little Bighorn.

George Crook: General who led the initial attacks against the Sioux in 1876.

Libby Custer: General Custer's wife, who accompanied him to the Dakotas and worked tirelessly after his death to burnish his reputation.

Ian Frazier: Author of *Great Plains,* a book about the Dakota territories, and *On the Rez,* a book about modern Oglala Sioux and his own wish to be called an Indian.

Ulysses S. Grant: Hero of the Civil War who, as president, authorized military action against the Sioux.

Russell Means: Twentieth-century Native American activist.

Red Cloud: Chief of one of the Oglala Sioux tribes at the Battle of Little Bighorn.

Red Star: An Arikara scout who accompanied Custer's regiment.

Marcus Reno: Battalion commander in the Seventh Cavalry. Major Reno survived the Little Bighorn engagement after being trapped for two days.

Alfred Terry: General Custer's superior officer in the campaign against the Sioux.

Wahsakie: Shoshone chief who aided the U.S. in its campaign against the Sioux.

Unit 7: William McKinley and the Spanish-American War

Emilio Aguinaldo: Leader of the Filipino independence movement.

William Jennings Bryan: Leader of the Democratic Party who opposed annexation of captured Spanish territory.

George Dewey: Admiral in command of the U.S. Far East naval squadron that sank the Spanish fleet in Manila Bay at the outbreak of the Spanish-American War, he also served on the U.S. commission set up to articulate American policy toward the Philippines.

William Randolph Hearst: Newspaper owner whose "yellow journalism" helped fire up the American public for war against Spain.

Arthur MacArthur: American general in charge of putting down Filipino insurrection after the war. He was the father of Douglas MacArthur, future general and World War II Pacific commander.

Thomas Reed: Republican speaker of the House of Representatives during the Spanish-American War. He opposed annexation and what he saw as imperialism.

Theodore Roosevelt: Avowed American imperialist who led a volunteer regiment in Cuba and supported the American annexation of the Philippines. He later became McKinley's vice president, then president when McKinley was assassinated by an anarchist.

Unit 8: Henry Ford and the American Worker

Harry Bennett: One of Henry Ford's closest associates and head of his private police force that enforced Ford's industrial, labor, and moral policies. He spearheaded Ford's efforts to prevent collective bargaining and unionization within his company's labor force.

James Couzens: Chief accountant and financial manager of the Ford Motor Company.

Thomas Edison: Famed inventor and patent holder. Henry Ford worked for him early in his career and was greatly influenced by him.

Ralph Waldo Emerson: Nineteenth-century transcendentalist writer and naturalist who, through the influence of his disciple, conservationist John Burroughs, became a strong influence on Ford.

Alex Malcolmsen: Coal merchant who became a partner in Ford's automobile company at its founding.

Charles Sorensen: Chief engineer and designer of the Ford Motor Company, best known for the Model T and for his design of large-scale integrated production processes.

Frederick Winslow Taylor: Engineer and writer who advocated the rationalization of industrial work processes. The philosophy became known as "Taylorism" and resulted in the assembly line.

Critical Thinking Using Primary Sources in U.S. History

Unit 9: Elizabeth Gurley Flynn and the Radical Labor Movement

Roger Baldwin: Founder of the American Civil Liberties Union to defend free speech from wartime restrictions. He was a friend of Elizabeth Gurley Flynn's and would later support Fred Korematsu's rights in the suits against Executive Order 9066.

Eugene V. Debs: Early labor leader and head of the American Socialist Party who was an early influence on Flynn. He ran for president in 1916 and was imprisoned for his opposition to America's entry into World War I. As Prisoner 9653, he ran again for president in 1919—from jail. He got a million votes. On Christmas day 1921, he received a presidential pardon and was released. He died in 1926.

Eugene Dennis: A chairman of the American Communist Party and associate of Elizabeth Gurley Flynn.

"Big" Bill Haywood: Leader of the syndicalist International Workers of the World trade union and an early influence on Elizabeth Gurley Flynn. He gave her her first job in a union.

J. Edgar Hoover: Director of the Bureau (later Federal Bureau) of Investigation. His willingness to see any movement for change as communist or communist-inspired allowed him to employ virtually any means to "protect" America from alien influence.

Joseph McCarthy: The Republican senator from Wisconsin who led the Senate Internal Security Committee hearings in the early 1950s. The hearings targeted communists and suspected "fellow travelers" in the U.S.

A. Mitchell Palmer: U.S. attorney general during the post-World War I Red Scare who targeted unions, radicals, and immigrants.

George Pettibone: Officer in the United Federation of Miners whom Elizabeth Gurley Flynn worked under early in her career.

John Reed: American socialist writer and war correspondent, friend of Elizabeth Gurley Flynn. He died in the Soviet Union during the Russian Civil War and was buried in the Kremlin Wall in Moscow.

Unit 10: Fred Korematsu and Japanese Internment

Roger Baldwin: Founder of the American Civil Liberties Union to defend free speech from wartime restrictions. He was a friend of Elizabeth Gurley Flynn's and supported Fred Korematsu's rights in the suits against Executive Order 9066.

Ernest Besig: Fred Korematsu's lawyer who argued his initial case in 1942.

Francis Biddle: Attorney general during the Roosevelt administration who opposed the exclusion act.

Ida Boitano: Fred Korematsu's girlfriend from 1938–1942.

General Delos Emmons: Military governor of Hawaii who refused to invoke Executive Order 9066.

Lieutenant General John DeWitt: General in command of the Western U.S. zone of operations, including California, who advocated the removal of civilians of Japanese descent.

Charles Fahy: Solicitor general in the Justice Department under Roosevelt who argued the case for exclusion before the Supreme Court.

J. Edgar Hoover: FBI director who, in February 1942, told Attorney General Biddle that the proposed mass exclusion of Jamanese Americans from the west coast on security grounds was not justifiable.

Peter Irons: Law professor and author who uncovered documents relating to the evacuation order and who worked on the 1982 case.

Franklin Roosevelt: President of the United States (1933–1945) who signed Executive Order 9066, the wartime exclusion act.

Henry Stimson: Secretary of war in the Roosevelt administration throughout World War II and a self-proclaimed expert on Japanese history and culture.

Unit 11: Harry S. Truman and the Dropping of the Atomic Bomb

Emperor Hirohito: Head of the Japanese government (though isolated from its daily operations), worshipped by the Japanese. His fate was a major issue in any peace settlement. His responsibility for Japanese wartime actions is hotly disputed.

Douglas MacArthur: General of the Army and Allied commander in the southwest Pacific theater in charge of a major "island-hopping" war effort against Japan. He later was Allied commander of all U.S. Army units in the Pacific. As supreme commander of the Allied powers in Japan, he supported its postwar recovery. He was also the first commander of the United Nations forces during the Korean War.

George Marshall: Chief of staff of the army and chairman of the Joint Chiefs of Staff. Marshall was Roosevelt's chief military adviser and became the first (five-star) general of the army. He argued against the bomb's use.

Vyacheslav Molotov: Stalin's foreign minister involved in negotiations regarding postwar settlements and the Russian entry into the war against Japan.

J. Robert Oppenheimer: The scientist in charge of the Manhattan Project—the development of the atomic bomb. He later came to oppose the development of the hydrogen bomb and lost his security clearance as a result.

Leo Szilard: The scientist who patented the atomic bomb process. Szilard wrote the letters that Einstein sent to Roosevelt to start the project and worked on it as a deterrent to German first-use. He cowrote a petition in 1945 protesting the planned use of the bomb against Japan.

Hideki Tojo: Leader of the militarist faction in Japan, war minister (1940–43), and premier (1941–44). General Tojo advocated a fight-to-the-last-man defense of Japan. At the end of the war, he tried, unsuccessfully, to commit suicide and was hanged as a war criminal by American occupation authorities in 1948.

Henry Wallace: Vice president until 1945 and chairman of Roosevelt's top policy group regarding development of the atomic bomb. Wallace was dropped from Roosevelt's 1944 reelection campaign in favor of Missouri Senator Harry S. Truman.

Unit 12: César Chávez and Migrant Farm Workers

Saul Alinsky: Union organizer who helped in the initial organization of farm workers in California.

Leroy Chatfield: Former wine maker who became an activist and organizer of the Immigrant Workers Organization.

Jim Drake: One of César Chávez's closest aides, who acted as his administrative assistant during the Delano strikes.

Frank Fitzsimmons: Head of the Teamsters Union during the Delano strikes who supported Nixon's stand against the United Farm Workers of America.

Wayne Hartmire: Migrant minister who volunteered to work with César Chávez.

Dolores Huerta: Chief negotiator for the United Farm Workers of America.

Donald Mcdonnel: Priest who educated César Chávez on the Catholic Church's stance on labor and unions.

Richard Nixon: President of the United States during the Delano strikes. He opposed unionization efforts.

Gilbert Padilla: Early farm worker organizer who joined Chávez and became vice president of the United Farm Workers of America.

Fred Ross: One of the organizers of the United Farm Workers of America. He started as a labor organizer during the Depression.

Unit 13: Gloria Steinem and the Women's Movement

Shirley Chisholm: The first African-American woman elected to Congress (D-NY).

Hillary Rodham Clinton: First lady of the United States from 1993 through 2000 and activist for women's causes.

Jerry Falwell: Founder of the "Moral Majority" and an opponent of the feminist movement.

Betty Friedan: Contemporary feminist and author of *The Feminine Mystique*.

Gerda Lerner: Writer on women's history and advocate of women's causes.

David McCullough: Historian, author, and host of public television's *American Experience* series.

Phyllis Schlafly: Conservative activist who opposed the feminist movement.

Donna Shalala: Member of the Clinton cabinet and an advocate on women's issues.

Share Your Bright Ideas with Us!

We want to hear from you! Your valuable comments and suggestions will help us meet your current and future classroom needs.

Your name_____Date_____

School name_____Phone_____

School address_____

Grade level taught_____Subject area(s) taught_____Average class size_____

Where did you purchase this publication?_____

Was your salesperson knowledgeable about this product?   Yes_____   No_____

What monies were used to purchase this product?

____School supplemental budget   ____Federal/state funding   ____Personal

Please "grade" this Walch publication according to the following criteria:

	A	B	C	D	F
Quality of service you received when purchasing	A	B	C	D	F
Ease of use	A	B	C	D	F
Quality of content	A	B	C	D	F
Page layout	A	B	C	D	F
Organization of material	A	B	C	D	F
Suitability for grade level	A	B	C	D	F
Instructional value	A	B	C	D	F

COMMENTS:_____

_____

What specific supplemental materials would help you meet your current—or future—instructional needs?

_____

Have you used other Walch publications? If so, which ones?_____

May we use your comments in upcoming communications?   ____Yes   ____No

Please **FAX** this completed form to **207-772-3105**, or mail it to:

Product Development, J. Weston Walch, Publisher, P.O. Box 658, Portland, ME 04104-0658

We will send you a **FREE GIFT** as our way of thanking you for your feedback. **THANK YOU!**